SANDBAG INTENSITY

THE FIFTY-REP SQUAT PROGRAM

CODY JANKO

Sandbag Intensity
The Fifty-Rep Squat Program

Copyright © 2025 Cody Janko

Published by Cody Janko
Kittredge, CO

For more information or to contact the author, please email cody.thestonecircle@gmail.com.

All rights reserved. No part of this book may be reproduced, distributed, or transmitted in any form or by any means, including photocopying, recording, or other electronic or mechanical methods, without the written permission from the publisher or author, except as permitted by U.S. copyright law or in the case of brief quotations embodied in a book review.

Disclaimer: Although the publisher and the author have made every effort to ensure that the information in this book was correct at press time and while this publication is designed to provide accurate information in regard to the subject matter covered, the publisher and the author assume no responsibility for errors, inaccuracies, omissions, or any other inconsistencies herein and hereby disclaim any liability to any party for any loss, damage, or disruption caused by errors or omissions, whether such errors or omissions result from negligence, accident, or any other cause.

ISBN 979-8-9985558-1-7 (softcover)
ISBN 979-8-9985558-2-4 (hardcover)
ISBN 979-8-9985558-0-0 (eBook)

Cover design: Abigael Elliott
Cover Illustration: Abigael Elliott
Interior Design by Ben Wolf, Inc.
Publishing services provided by BelieversBookServices.com

First printing: 2025

Printed in the United States of America

*For The Stone Circle community.
Thanks for being awesome.*

CONTENTS

Author's Note   vii

1. Intensity and Drive   1
2. High-Rep Squats   11
3. Strength-Endurance   15
4. Calisthenics Circuits   25
5. The Bear Hug Carry   31
6. Program Introduction   37
7. The Sandbag Box Squat   47
8. Sandbag Workouts   53
9. Calisthenics Workouts   67
10. Box Squat Tips   83
11. Sandbag Intensity   93
12. Alternate Programs   97

About the Author   123
Endnotes   125

AUTHOR'S NOTE

In the months leading up to writing this book, I managed to squat a 250-pound sandbag for a set of 50 reps, a 220-pound sandbag for a set of 100 reps, a 200-pound sandbag for a set of 200 reps, and a 175-pound sandbag for a set of 300 reps—all while weighing under 170 pounds myself. I also completed multiple 350+ rep calisthenics circuits in under 20 minutes and made it through my first ever 25-mile hike up and down the side of a mountain.

Why would anyone do these things?

Why would someone want to?

That's what *Sandbag Intensity* is about.

Motivation. Mindset. Perspective.

The beauty of exercise for the sake of itself, the joy of doing something extreme, and the life-changing effects that come with pushing the limits of what's possible.

At the end of this book, you'll find what I consider the ultimate high-rep sandbag training program—the exact program I used to accomplish these crazy feats. It's designed to rapidly increase strength-endurance, muscle size, overall conditioning, and the power of the mind.

The program gave me an entirely new understanding of what it means to push myself, and my training will never be the same. I think you'll like it.

More than anything I hope this book motivates you to go lift some heavy weights, because that's what it's all about!

Thanks for reading.
-Cody

1

INTENSITY AND DRIVE

The Neighbor

Life was peaceful before he got his Stone Cold Steve Austin T-shirt.

Monday it's video games and a birthday party, Tuesday he attacks me with a folding chair on the front lawn.

No real damage done, he could hardly hold the thing.

That was the start, and his creativity only grew.

Sneak attacks from behind the tree.

Bodyslams off the roof.

A battle charge with a steel trash can.

It was that last one that did it. For some reason the trash can got to me and I officially had my very first goal: learn to fight back.

After some careful thought, my seven-year-old mind created the ultimate training program.

Step One: Flare your traps like Goldberg every couple minutes.

Step Two: Fight invisible enemies while doing cool parkour moves on the living room couch.

Step Three: Run circles around the yard and the garage.
Step Four: Repeat daily until victory is achieved.

Months went by and still I lost.
My couch acrobatics and Goldberg intimidation tactics were nothing compared with his cunning.
False peace offerings.
"Don't worry, we can be on the same team today."
Promises of cool loot.
"No really, this time I just want to show you the rock I found."
Pretend family gatherings.
"My dad said you can come over for dinner. It's okay, you can let your guard down."
Defeat after defeat, from The People's Elbow to The Stone Cold Stunner, through it all I held onto my goal.
I kept training.
Until one day it happened.
He came at me going for a piledriver, and I managed to slip behind him and wrap my arm around his throat. From there I tripped him forward and performed a kind of bodyslam. After that all I had to do was use my superior weight to hold him in place until he gave up and accepted defeat.
It was an unbeatable move, and I never lost again.

Uncertainty

The worst part of training for muscle is uncertainty. Adding mass is a slow process, and it's impossible to gauge progress on a daily scale. Even a month is often too short a time to notice real changes in muscle size.
Uncertainty.

"Am I actually doing enough?"

"I seem to be getting stronger, but what if I chose the wrong exercises?"

"Am I using the correct rep range?"

"Am I under-recovered, or under-trained?"

The uncertainty leads to fear, and fear kills gains. Unable to trust the process a lifter moves from one program to the next, never pushing any one thing far enough to see results. Eventually he ends up plateaued, muscle and strength gain at a complete standstill.

Many reach this place and never leave it.

Caught up in the details.

Trying every program.

Constantly studying every possible thing there is to study on exercise and never making it anywhere.

Year after year consistently showing up to the gym, stuck right at the borderline between average and exceptional.

With so much information available it's easy to assume the solution must be a complicated one. If you can just dig deep enough you'll find that one thing you've been missing. The secret method is out there somewhere. It has to be!

Nothing works.

"I guess I'm just not good enough."

That's exactly the position I was in myself. For years I trained without fail, never making it anywhere. I went on extreme bulks, gaining ridiculous amounts of fat just to end up back in the same place I had started a year later. I tried every diet and specialty program. No matter what I did I couldn't seem to make any gains.

That was until I discovered the truth.

The problem never had to do with programs or diets, or anything of the sort.

The problem was me.

Intensity

Intensity.
    Effort.
    The missing piece.
    Without intensity a permanent plateau is inevitable.
    With intensity however, uncertainty goes away.
    Intensity is THE THING standing between you and a breakthrough where results happen seemingly all at once.
    It cuts through every other insignificant training variable and guarantees progress will be made.

Intensity:
The level or extent of strength or force that something possesses.
Extreme emotional excitement.

    Intensity is concentration; vigor. It's the power of the mind, and it's an ability that can be trained.
    Tapping into it won't be easy. You'll need complete and undivided focus during your workouts. You'll need what might at first seem an absurd and unnecessary level of effort. You'll need to push yourself to the point where you can say with honest sincerity, "I have nothing left to give."
    That's what it takes.
    Once you learn to harness true intensity, suddenly everything becomes easy. Muscle, strength, whatever other attribute you're after—it's yours for the taking.
    From a standstill to flying. That's what intensity can do for you.

Okay, well how do you get it?

Just 'try harder'?

Yes and no.

I believe the answer is found in drive, in the will to succeed —the NEED. When you have the desire to succeed at a goal above all other things in life, regardless of what it takes, that's where true intensity is found.

Here's the trick:

Even when muscle growth is the goal, I do not believe it's the best way forward. To reach the intensity level needed to build lots of muscle, I believe you need a goal that goes beyond muscle.

You need something more, something more tangible.

Like the young boy who trained every day, running around his yard because he wanted with everything he had to defeat the neighbor kid who wouldn't stop using him as a pro-wrestling practice dummy, so too must you find something that drives you forward.

Competition always helps. If you can find it that's great, but I believe the desire to defeat your current self can be equally as effective. With that in mind, the path to extreme muscle gain becomes clear.

All you need to do is choose a skill or a sport with a high potential for strength gain—one you find exciting—and get to work.

Many go to powerlifting or strongman, CrossFit, or Olympic lifting for this exact reason. What ignited that fire in me and allowed me to tap into the intensity I was lacking was lifting heavy sandbags.

It seems such a simple thing. Pick up the bag of sand. Put it down. Repeat. It's tough to say why exactly I find it so enjoyable, but for whatever reason I just do.

I'll never forget the first time I successfully lifted a sandbag to my shoulder. It was like being a kid again. It was pure joy. I felt I had found my purpose.

Honest Genuine Joy

When I was in the sixth grade I was hooked on a video game called RuneScape. It was a massive online game where you played alongside others to level up your character. There were tons of different skills you could choose to work on, but my favorite was mining. Mining was a basic skill and there wasn't much to it—buy a pickaxe, find a rock, click on it, get the ore, repeat. Looking back, mining in RuneScape seems just as pointless as lifting a bag of sand is, but I was obsessed with it.

I had a friend who also played the game, Kurt. I'd see him in the halls between classes at school, sneak up beside him and say the word 'iron' and he would let out this groan of sadness. It was the perfect prank, reminding him how long he still had to wait until he could go home and play the game again.

RuneScape dominated every aspect of my life. All day I would think about it. If I had access to a computer at school I'd read about it online, looking up information on quests or different kinds of armor. When I was home I'd play it late into the night. It was this constant positive force that filled me with complete happiness. It was something to look forward to. It didn't matter how the rest of the day went, with RuneScape there waiting for me I could get through anything.

As we get older and responsibilities pile up, that honest, genuine joy seems to fade. It's often difficult to find it at all, let alone to have something that sticks with you for months on end. When I first lifted a sandbag, it was like being that young kid mining for ore again. Right then I knew it would guide my life. Every training session became like a game. The time I wasn't lifting sandbags I was reading about it or watching videos of others, learning from their technique. For the first time in so many years I found myself jumping out of bed in the morning excited to go train.

Heavy sandbag lifting gave my life a purpose beyond bodybuilding, and following that purpose built me a lot of muscle.

I believe this is the true secret to developing the drive to succeed, and in turn a higher level of intensity. Find something that consumes you, something you can't help but think about constantly. When you have that, effort becomes easy. The intensity comes naturally. Muscle is inevitable.

Infinite Potential

In addition to pushing you further by making progress something you enjoy, there's another aspect to lifting sandbags that I believe makes them special:

The potential for pushing sandbags to an extreme level is nearly infinite.

Most sandbag exercises are near-complete, full-body movements, and with so much muscle involved at once, it almost always feels like you have more to give.

Compare this with a bicep curl.

Pick up a dumbbell, lock into a preacher station, and curl the weight until the biceps wear out.

Simple and straightforward.

Now stand up and use a bit of body English to lift the dumbbell.

You can push the set much further.

Finally switch to a barbell and use your hips and arms and legs to complete the rep. With so much muscle involved it feels like you always have more to give. You will eventually reach failure and have to stop, but the potential to keep throwing that weight around is sky-high.

Sandbags are like that taken to the extreme. Every sandbag exercise involves nearly every muscle of the body, meaning if you have the will, there is likely a way to do more reps.

If you can do 5 reps, you can probably do 6.

If you can carry a sandbag for 30 seconds, you can probably go for 35.

With sandbags you can almost always push just a little further if you have the mental strength for it. Sandbags give you the opportunity to rapidly increase your tolerance to high-intensity work. They're a direct path to improving your ability to push beyond your own perceived limits. With sandbags, intensity becomes second nature.

When looking at the exercises you can do with a sandbag, one stands out above the rest as having nearly infinite potential to push beyond the ordinary stopping point: the box squat.

2

HIGH-REP SQUATS

Breathing Squats

Sandbag Intensity uses the high-rep sandbag box squat as its foundation. While I do believe the program is unique in its overall approach to exercise, it's impossible to miss the obvious influence, 20-rep barbell breathing squats. Used for decades, notably in the book *Super Squats* by Randall Strossen, 20-rep breathing squats are a time-tested method for packing on tons of mass. The core idea of the 20-rep squat program is taking a weight you could normally squat for a hard set of 10, and forcing yourself to do 20 without ever racking the bar. You do this by resting between reps, taking as many deep breaths as you need before continuing on.

I mention this now as a way to pay respect to that program. It's perfect as is, and I encourage anyone who hasn't tried it to do so at some point.

Sandbag Intensity is neither an attempt to improve nor replace the basic 20-rep breathing squat program, rather it's something different entirely.

A Complete Rest

When squatting a barbell you're under constant tension during the entire set. Although you can rest your legs at the top of every rep, your body must still work to support the bar on your back. This is in many ways a net positive, and is undoubtedly responsible for a sizable portion of the muscle gain one experiences from high-rep breathing squats, but the constant tension also acts as a kind of cap. You can squat 20 reps with your 10-rep max as the program suggests, maybe even 25 if you're extremely conditioned to the work, but there's only so long you can support a heavy weight on your back. There's a limit to how far you can go.

The sandbag box squat doesn't have this problem. Rather than unending, constant tension, the bottom of every rep is a place of rest. This means the only limit to how far you can take a set is the strength of your mind. You can always recover just enough to do another rep, even when using very heavy sandbags—you just have to make yourself do it.

With this in mind, the primary objective of the *Sandbag Intensity* program is working up to squatting your 10-rep max for 50 reps. That may sound extreme, unnecessary even, but with the sandbag box squat it is well within the realm of possible. More on that later.

The Set Itself

Another difference between *Sandbag Intensity* and the 20-rep breathing squat program is its approach to building muscle. Where *Super Squats* is focused on muscle as the main objective, "How To Gain 30 Pounds Of Muscle In 6 Weeks," *Sandbag Inten-*

sity views the set itself as the goal. It views high-rep box squats as something worth doing, not because the benefits you get from them are as extreme as the idea of squatting a 10-rep max for 50 reps is (they are), but because the pursuit of something profound gives life purpose.

The muscle will come, of course it will—this is heavy weight and high reps we're talking about here—but the primary objective of the program is accomplishing something extreme. Going where no one has gone before. Shattering the barrier and raising the ceiling of possibility so high as to make anyone who witnesses what you've done question if they're actually training hard enough, or just going through the motions. It's about proving to yourself you have what it takes. High-rep sandbag box squats become your sport, they give you a goal that goes beyond muscle, and in doing so they build a lot of it.

In addition to muscle, the high-rep sandbag box squat also gives you what I believe is the single greatest attribute a person can train for: strength-endurance.

3

STRENGTH-ENDURANCE

The Commute

January.
    Two hours pre-civil twilight.
    The snowfall has stopped.
    The sky is clear.
Moving in a kind of semi-synthetic harmony,
Moonlight and starlight and lamp post light pass together through the fresh-powder crystals ornamenting the earth,
Casting a tangible glow,
Creating an atmosphere both day-like in its visibility,
And yet somehow darker than ordinary night.
It was time to go.

Three miles along city streets, five miles along the creek, two miles on the streets again.

Yesterday's sun shone just hot enough, and for just long enough to melt the previous night's snow down to a slushy mess before the freeze set in and the next snow hit, creating a thick layer of uneven ice beneath the newly fallen top layer.

The trek would be slow going.

I was on my bike, an old Gary Fisher that had been with the family for decades. It came with me a year prior when I left home, twelve hours west for the city.

Three miles, five miles, two miles.

That was my daily commute to work at the dog kennel.

Rain was always the worst; at least it wasn't raining. With rain came invisible potholes and wet clothes. I'd take the snow any day. Snow did take more effort though, and on a day like this one—new snow covering new ice—every turn of the pedals would only amount to a half-turn of the tires as the slick ground sapped away all traction.

The ice also meant lots of walking. If I had learned one thing over the previous months, it was that even the shortest downhill stretch represented a potential for black ice and a wipeout. Cracked ribs heal slowly.

Three miles, five miles, two miles.

In conditions like this, the first stretch was always the most challenging physically. Not yet quite fully awake, my mind would be mostly turned off to the knowledge of how far I actually had to go, but for that I almost felt every turn of the pedals that much more.

Five minutes in, my legs are on fire.

Ten minutes gone, my lungs are too.

Twenty minutes, and even my arms and back are feeling the effects of the constant pull on the handlebars.

So much effort for what felt like such little distance gained.

I just had to keep going.

I was moving, and that counted for something.

Push the pedals.

Pull the handlebars.

Don't stop.

Three miles down, onto the five-mile stretch along the almost forest-like frozen creek path. There were streets nearby, but in those early hours through the snow the ride almost felt like an expedition through a mountain pass.

It was at this point my mind would become fully awake.

This caused a few things to happen.

First was the knowledge of how much further I had to go, and how much effort I still had to give. With a clear mind the truth always surfaces, try as I might to stop it. After making my way through what already felt like so much, I was only just getting started.

The second thing to happen is I would begin to reflect on my situation. There I was out in the freezing cold pushing my body to its limit, doing something no one else was while the world slept. There's something peaceful about that, encouraging even.

Making my way past empty streets usually packed bumper to bumper with traffic.

Houses and apartment buildings, offices with unlit windows.

A path along the creek usually crawling with people completely untouched.

I would think back on all the countless hours spent longing for adventure and realize I had finally made it.

"This is it."

There's a sense of purpose that comes with that realization, of pride, and pride is a powerful emotion. It overrides any feelings of doubt you might have. When you truly believe what you're doing has meaning, you will get it done.

I wasn't just making my way to work, pushing in extreme conditions for a minimum-wage check.

No.

I was a trailblazer, out there creating the path that would soon guide hundreds.

Me, the unmarked road and the spinning of the tires—I was a pioneer.

Invigorated by my new sense of purpose, the five-mile stretch along the creek would pass by almost too soon and it was back to the city streets.

Three and five miles down, two to go.

The final stretch always seemed like it should be the breaking point.

I was exhausted and everything hurt.

It never was.

There's a feeling that comes over you when you've passed beyond what's ordinary.

You've already done something great, all that's left is to finish.

At this point you might begin to feel just a bit wild.

Your mind enters a place like pure instinct.

Nothing else exists.

The physical fatigue you feel is meaningless.

You've made it this far, you can make it the rest of the way.

All doubt has gone.

Pedal.

Stop for the occasional passing car or snow plow.

Pedal.

Hop off the bike and walk down the small hill.

Pedal.

Carry the bike over the still breakable semi-frozen puddle formed where the sidewalk meets the street.

Push on the pedals, pull on the handlebars, keep going.

Ten miles done.

Back to reality.

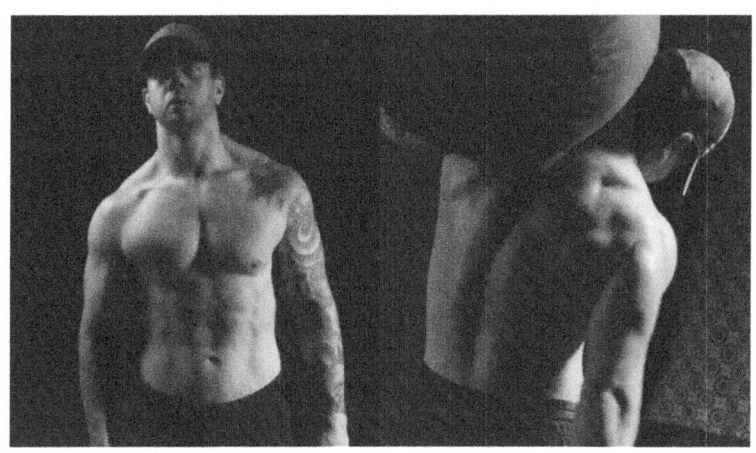

Strength-Endurance

Strength-endurance is the strength to endure hardship in any environment. It's a representation of the desire to live, to go on living, and the love of life. Someone with true strength-endurance looks at the hard parts of existence and smiles. He delights in the glory of challenge, of everything that isn't mundane and comfortable.

Strength-endurance is the strength of an adventurer, a traveler, an explorer and a leader. It's the strength of a valuable and useful person.

Strength-endurance is the strength to move stone or lumber all day in the construction of a shelter.

It's the strength to carry an injured person to safety from somewhere 5 miles deep in the woods, to trek 15 miles through waist-deep snow with an 80-pound pack, to scale a mountain after falling, and to keep fighting when it would be so much easier to give up.

An epic feat of strength-endurance is like a journey. Filled with different stages of hardship and struggle, marked by countless opportunities to take the easy way out and quit, for those with the will, strength-endurance is the path of the hero.

It's the attribute we were made to have, and having it is wonderful.

The Bodybuilder

There are many paths you can take to develop strength-endurance. When I look at exercise though, I can't help but view it through the lens of a bodybuilder. Muscle gain must be considered. If I'm going to commit to a training style it must place the muscles under a high level of tension, and it must allow for continuous progressive overload.

What then is the perfect middle ground?

Where is balance found?

That's what *Sandbag Intensity* is all about. The high-rep sandbag box squat, and the calisthenics circuit. The epic quest through the early-morning snow and heavy strength training both.

Extreme Sets

The sandbag box squat starts off easy. You take a weight you could normally squat for 10 reps, and rest-pause your way to 15. Not so bad. Over time though, each set becomes something so much more than that.

Sets of 70 reps lasting 10 minutes.

Sets of 170 lasting 20 if you decide to take it that far.

During every set you face constant uncertainty and doubt.

You against a seemingly insurmountable foe.

10 reps and the physical exhaustion starts to kick in.

20 reps and the mind starts to wonder how it ever thought a set of 100 was possible to begin with.

30 reps and the arms and legs start to burn.

35 and the back does too.

50 down and every rep leaves you breathless, as if you just ran a 4-minute mile.

60 reps and you enter a place of pure will and determination.

The mind hardens itself to the work, the body does what's required.

70 reps and maybe you start to feel a bit of hope, only 30 more to go.

75 and that hope is crushed, the final battle has begun.

Between every rep is a 10-second fight against the desire to quit.

You keep going.

You're doing something important.

This has meaning.

Deep breath.

Brace the core.

Squeeze the sandbag.

Stand up.

Flex the glutes.

Sit down.

Deep breath.

Deep breath.

Repeat.

Eventually you make it to the end of the set. You got the extra reps. You pushed further than you ever have before. You just did a hundred-rep set with a heavy weight and you're a changed person for it. Every set, and every rep within that set is a condensed journey of strength-endurance.

On the grand scale, each 'set' constitutes a 'rep' in the totality of the month and the year. It's one thing to make it through a set once, on a single day. To keep going week after week, set and rep after set and rep—that's the real journey.

You'll find as time passes you begin to look forward to it.
The struggle.
That moment of hopelessness 60 reps in.
It becomes the place where you feel most alive.
You keep pushing.
A wanderer in undiscovered territory writing the map.
Raising the ceiling of possibility until the roof disappears completely and all that's left is the open night sky.
Months go by, the seasons change, and so too do you change.
No longer do the usual stressors of life cause you trouble.
Nothing that once felt difficult carries weight.
Like the hero returned to a peaceful existence after a seemingly hopeless adventure, you'll find joy in the life you have.
Things aren't so bad.
You know what it feels like to struggle.

The calisthenics circuit follows a similar path. You choose your exercises and rep scheme, and the first few workouts don't cause you much trouble. You beat your previous record by many seconds—often minutes at first—but as time goes by you begin to realize what it truly takes to improve.

This is not a passive quest.
You cannot coast through and hope for change.
One round done, how are your muscles already so worn out?
Two rounds and it's hard to breathe.
Three rounds and your entire being is concentrated on keeping up the pace.
Four rounds and you've done it.
It took everything you had, but you managed to beat your

previous record by 6 seconds. It seems impossible to think you tried nearly this hard last time but the numbers don't lie. It's only going to get harder, but you'll learn to love it. Every workout is a reminder of what you're capable of.

You have more to give.

4

CALISTHENICS CIRCUITS

The Failed Bulk

Many years ago I decided to try a popular 3x5 barbell squat focused program. I had been plateaued for years at that point, strength and muscle both stuck, so I figured committing to a time-tested routine made sense.

Squats: Three sets of five reps, three times a week.

Milk: A gallon and a half every single day.

The program had a few other exercises too, but squats and milk were the main focus.

Things were fine at first. I greatly improved my squat technique, and my strength grew rapidly. About a month in though, I started having some issues.

First and foremost was the program itself. I had already been training for years at that point, and while I wasn't particularly strong, it didn't take long for me to max out the gains I could make from a beginner program like that. I should have moved onto an intermediate program after that first month, but I didn't know any better at the time. I just kept pushing. Trying and failing to improve my sets of five. Resetting with a lower weight before working up to the same plateau and failing again. Eventually the only thing driving me forward was my rapid weight gain.

The second issue was the milk. A gallon and a half every single day for a 142-pound person was way too much. A month in and I had already lost all definition in my muscles.

After 3 months I couldn't take it any longer. My squat was much stronger, though not nearly as strong as it could have been had I switched programs when it was time. That part was great, but I had to stop. Constant sets of 5 day after day had destroyed my love for the iron. I was completely burnt out.

I was also fat and it showed. I pushed into obese territory for the first time in my life, and I was miserable. My squat had improved, but I had added nearly fifty pounds of pure fat to make it happen.

I was in the worst shape of my life.

I couldn't live like that.

Strength be damned, I needed to drop the weight.

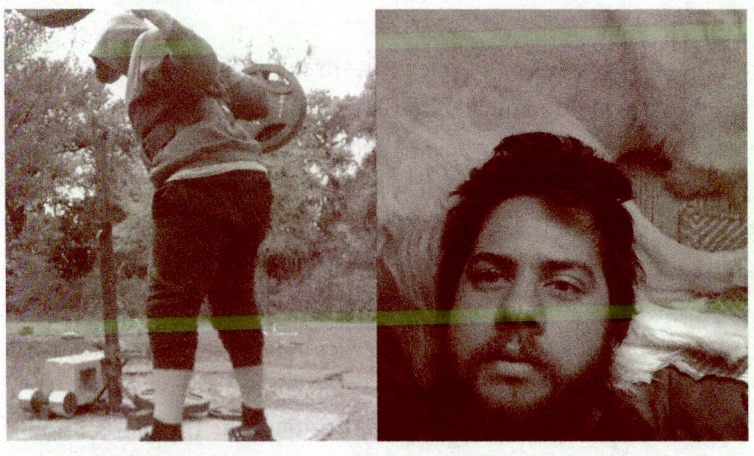

Density Training

Because I was done with barbells for the moment, I decided to become a full-time calisthenics guy. The change in training style wasn't enough though. After sets of five for months on end, the thought of counting reps in the normal way made my stomach turn. That's when I remembered a training style known as "density training."

I had first read about it years before in a book called *Muscle Logic: Escalating Density Training* by author Charles Staley.

In the book, Staley made an argument for the use of training density as a form of progressive overload. Rather than increasing weight or reps with the typical "three sets per exercise" setup, you would pick a set time limit—10 minutes for example—and do as many reps as you could in that time, with the goal of doing more reps every workout, thus increasing the density of your training.

I found it very enjoyable, but it wasn't quite what I was looking for at the time. While I liked the idea of density, I wanted something that was as focused on endurance and cardio as it was on building muscle. I was fat and got winded walking on flat ground, I needed something more.

Balance

Eventually I landed on an idea that would lay the framework of my training for the next year. Increasing density would be the goal, but rather than more work in a set time limit, I would do the same amount of work in less time. Rather than X number of reps in 10 minutes, I would do X reps faster every workout.

In addition to that, rather than focusing on only one exercise at a time—essentially doing one giant rest-pause set—I would use four or five exercises, each based on one of the upper-body movement patterns.

    Horizontal push.
    Horizontal pull.
    Vertical push.
    Vertical pull.
    Abs (not technically a movement pattern, but you get the idea).

I would choose a set number of reps, and rotate through each exercise until I completed every one. This setup kept the muscles close to failure at all times, and allowed me to move through the circuit without ever needing to rest. Nonstop movement meant a great endurance challenge, and keeping the muscles close to failure meant gains.

    Balance.

Originally I focused on a "10 down" rep scheme, which is 10 reps of each exercise, then 9, 8, 7, all the way down to 1.

    10, 9, 8, 7, 6, 5, 4, 3, 2, 1

I later progressed to a "10 down and up" as I called it, 10-1-1-10.

    10, 9, 8, 7, 6, 5, 4, 3, 2, 1, 1, 2, 3, 4, 5, 6, 7, 8, 9, 10

I created a few different circuits using this setup. My favorite was made up of towel pull-ups, dips, ring rows, decline pike push-ups, and the ab wheel rollout.

At first I was very slow. A basic "10 down" with that circuit took me nearly an hour to complete the first time I tried it. I was so out of shape I couldn't catch my breath. I stuck with it though, and the results were beyond anything I could have hoped for. I was seeing noticeable changes in body composition on a daily basis, and after just three months of intense training I was lean again.

Over the following year I took that basic "10 down" circuit from a starting point of nearly an hour, to just over 30 minutes using a "10 down and up" rep scheme.

For reference, a "10 down and up" circuit made up of 5 different exercises is 550 reps total!

I went from the worst shape of my life to the absolute best. I had more endurance than when I ran cross-country as a kid. Significantly more than when I was lean and lifting barbells. I felt like I had endless energy, like I could run stairs nonstop all day if I wanted to. I had insane strength-endurance and control over my own body. Never before had I seen such dramatic results in such a short amount of time. Calisthenics circuits changed everything.

5

THE BEAR HUG CARRY

Dinosaur Training

It's interesting how quickly a thing turns invisible.
The book you always meant to read left forever open to page 4 on the dining-room table.
The shirt meant for the hamper which, in a hurried moment, was tossed just a bit too far to the left and has since taken up residence on the floor by the closet.
The cup on the dresser.
These things become part of the backdrop, the scenery, and in no time at all you cease to remember they weren't meant to go there to begin with.
Sometimes the opposite happens.
You decide you need something and there it is. Like a shadow on the wall suddenly solidified that old dress shirt turns up at exactly the moment you need it.
It was a moment like that when I first experienced for myself the true power of the bear hug carry. I had recently finished reading a particularly exciting chapter in a book called *Dinosaur Training*, where author Brooks Kubik recounted an epic tale of

the day he and his training partners took a heavy odd-object carry to complete failure. The story ends with each of them sprawled out on the ground gasping for air. For some reason that sounded like the exact kind of thing I wanted to go through myself, the problem was I didn't have anything worth carrying.

After finishing that chapter I took my dogs out to the backyard, and there it was. On the ground propped up against the fence was a stone. A year living at the place and never once had I noticed it. It didn't look like a very good stone for carrying. It was oddly shaped and had a sharp edge along one side. It didn't look very heavy either (I later weighed it at just 75 pounds), but it was there, and it was the closest thing I had to a heavy odd-object. Also, standing there looking at the stone, for some reason I couldn't help but feel it wanted to be lifted. So I did.

I quickly realized the oddly shaped rock wasn't heavy enough to push in the same way Brooks had in his book—floored after just a few minutes—so I decided I would go for time. I set the stopwatch on my phone, lifted the stone, and started walking back and forth in my yard. I began with something resembling a zercher position, switched to a bear hug, and alternated between carrying it on each shoulder before starting the cycle again. Every time one spot became too much to handle I'd move to something else, and I just kept going until somehow 30 minutes had passed.

Initially I felt a bit let down if I'm being completely honest. The book made carrying an odd-object seem like this amazing thing, and after 30 straight minutes I felt underwhelmed. Of course the problem was the stone just wasn't heavy enough, but I walked away from that workout wishing I'd stuck to my regular routine, more than a little disappointed in myself for following the shiny object once again.

Extreme Muscle Soreness

An hour later after dinner and a shower I started to notice something strange. It was my legs. For the first time in years I had what felt like intense growing pains in my legs—like I was in the seventh grade again going through some kind of puberty-induced growth spurt.

Half an hour after that I began to feel a deep ache in the spaces between the bones of my hands. Extending my fingers caused a feeling much like that first stretch of the back after a long night's sleep.

Years spent lifting weights and never once had I felt anything quite like it.

Not long after that I reached my arm to the side to grab the nearby TV remote and the power of the odd-object carry hit me with full force. Everything all at once. Twisting my body ignited a fire in my core unlike anything I had ever experienced from training. I suddenly became aware of what seemed like a hundred small muscles I hadn't previously known were there.

Side note: When I was 10 years old, some friends and I thought it would be a smart idea to follow a path over some fallen barbed wire along a cliff ledge. It was muddy that day, and I ended up falling pretty far. I broke my left wrist and my right ankle, but the worst part was the internal bruising I had on the right side of my stomach. Any kind of movement caused intense pain. I won't say the soreness I felt in my core after carrying the stone quite reached that level, but it was a lot closer than I thought was possible from exercise.

I also felt the soreness in my arms. Moving my wrists caused my forearms to cramp uncontrollably. My upper arms felt sore down to the bone, much like my legs. I'd done my share of heavy cheat curls and rows, and weighted, stretch-focused exercises for the upper arms at that point, but I was not prepared for what I felt at that moment.

My back too. My lats and traps, and every other muscle of the upper back. I typically like upper back soreness, but this was almost too much. Like the ache you get during that brief moment of clarity two days deep into a fever dream, it just hurt.

I also felt something completely unexpected, my pecs. A couple years prior I had done some extremely heavy weighted pull-up negatives and ended up with the most intense pec soreness I'd ever experienced. It was like every fiber was completely torn in the best kind of way. This was a lot like that.

When I stood up I felt my hamstrings and glutes too. It felt like the day after some high-volume reverse lunges. Those always make me extremely sore the next day. Somehow carrying the stone got me to that place in just a few hours.

The Wrestler

Needless to say from that moment on I was a believer. That night I ordered my first strongman style sandbag, and the next day I made my own makeshift bag with some rocks from the yard, a few contractor trash bags, and a canvas bag I found at the nearby thrift store labeled 'Mom's Best Day Out.'

There were a few sandbag movements I liked, but nothing hooked me more than the bear hug carry. I believe it's the ultimate exercise, and I credit it with eventually pushing me past the muscle and strength plateau I had been stuck on for years at that point.

The immediate effects were extreme, but the changes I felt after a few months with the exercise were even more profound. I started to notice a change in the way I held myself, in the way I walked around going through the day, and in how I felt.

The best way I can describe it is to have you picture a state champion college wrestler on the mat. Look at how he stands and the way he moves. Something about it just gives you the impression that no matter how hard you tried, even if you attacked him unaware, you could never unbalance him even the slightest bit.

That's how I felt.

My stride changed. The positioning of my torso changed. My slightly internally rotated shoulder posture went away, as did my slightly forward head posture. I felt more balanced and confident in my positioning in space. The bear hug carry made me like a wrestler; sturdy and solid, agile and nimble.

That feeling has only improved over the years. The bear hug carry is in my opinion the single greatest exercise there is. There's nothing else like it, and any program that doesn't feature it is missing out.

6

PROGRAM INTRODUCTION

Minimalist Program, Maximum Results

The *Sandbag Intensity* program is designed to rapidly increase strength-endurance, muscle size, overall conditioning, and the power of the mind. It's one of a kind, and I've yet to see anything else quite like it.

At the heart of the program is the high-rep sandbag box squat. You can think of it as the power source that feeds everything else. The further you push the box squat, the stronger the current, the brighter the signal, the more adaptation you'll see everywhere.

The high-rep sandbag box squat makes extreme intensity accessible to anyone.

It acts as a sort of guarantee.

Make yourself push further, get the extra reps every workout, and you can rest assured knowing you're on the right track.

No longer must you deal with the uncertainty that comes with training for a purpose.

"Am I doing the right thing to make my muscles grow?"

"Is my conditioning actually improving?"

"Did I really get stronger, or did I just somehow cheat the system?"

That all goes away.

With the box squat you take complete control over the outcome.

It's on you now, you're in charge.

High-rep sandbag box squats are so effective, I sincerely believe they have the power to supercharge any training program. You don't need to follow the *Sandbag Intensity* program if you don't like it. Take the box squat and create something of your own if that's what you want to do.

That being said a lot of work went into creating *Sandbag Intensity*. Make no mistake, high-rep box squats will bury you if you aren't careful. High reps with heavy weight and a high frequency means you walk a very fine line at all times between rapid progress, and pushing beyond your recovery capacity. In a program like this, everything must have a purpose.

The most difficult part in creating *Sandbag Intensity* was cutting out everything that wasn't absolutely essential, while also covering as many bases as I could. There are endless possibilities for exercise combinations. I believe I've found the most effective one for becoming a master of strength-endurance, while building a lot of muscle in the process.

Sandbag Intensity is a highly specialized program. It's minimalist in nature, and doesn't cover every aspect of movement. What it does do is make sure nothing falls behind. If you move from a general sandbag routine and run *Sandbag Intensity* for a few months, you'll find that when you go back to a more diverse program you won't have lost anything.

This part was very important to me. Power, and the sandbag-to-shoulder are a few of my favorite things. When creating this strength-endurance program (which operates on an entirely different system compared to a program centered on building power), I had to be sure it wouldn't train me to be less powerful.

It didn't.

When running the program I went months without ever doing a single sandbag-to-shoulder attempt, or any kind of explosive lifting from the lap. When I did eventually go back to the sandbag-to-shoulder I was able to pick up right where I had left off, while also feeling much stronger, and more 'solid' than I ever had before. After a few sessions spent practicing technique, I found my power level had actually increased by a lot. The *Sandbag Intensity* program built my base so wide, everything that once challenged me became easy.

This is a specialty, minimalist program, but the results you get from it are maximal.

The Exercises

When setting up the program I kept a few things in mind:

1. Is it possible to recover from this?
2. Will this program lead to any glaring weak points?
3. Will this lead to overuse injuries, and how can I ward against them?
4. Will this lead to mental burnout?
5. I want to challenge the mind so it grows stronger, but how much is too much?
6. Will this build strength in at least most of the basic movement patterns?
7. Will this build muscle everywhere?

When selecting exercises for the program, each one had to fit a list of criteria:

1. Does this enhance the box squat in some way?
2. Will this help to ward off injury in some way?
3. Does this fix a potential gap in strength?
4. Does this build a lot of muscle over a large area?
5. Does this improve multiple things at once?

It took some experimentation, but I believe I've discovered the best possible setup.

Each sandbag exercise builds overall strength and muscle, and enhances the box squat in some way, while also making sure you don't become too much of a specialist. You'll walk away from this program strong, and ready for anything.

The One-Motion Lift From The Ground To The Chest

The one-motion lift from the ground to the chest does a few things very well.

1. It improves strength off the ground

Lifting heavy sandbags from the ground can be very fatiguing, more so than most other sandbag exercises. This is a huge potential problem in a program like this, where managing fatigue is so important. Too much time spent lifting heavy sandbags from the ground would make the program unusable. At the same time, the last thing we want is for that strength to fall behind. The program will have failed if it leaves you with a weakness there. The one-motion lift from the ground to the chest is the perfect solution. It lets you continue building your max strength off the ground with lighter weights, thus reducing overall fatigue.

2. It forces you to be powerful and explosive through a large range of motion

Even though *Sandbag Intensity* is focused on building strength-endurance, we don't want our explosive power level to fall behind. The one-motion lift from the ground to the chest is a good way to sneak in some extra work for that, without taking away from the rest of the program.

Beginning a workout with the exercise also acts as a wake-up call for the central nervous system, priming you for what comes next.

The Row

The sandbag row is the perfect counter to the sandbag box squat.

1. It builds strength off the ground

The sandbag row has direct carryover to the lift from the ground. Alongside the one-motion lift from the ground to the chest, prioritizing the row in the program lets us build that strength without needing to spend much time on it directly, reducing overall fatigue.

2. It builds a lot of muscle

The sandbag row is possibly the greatest sandbag muscle building exercise there is. It will add a lot of size to the hamstrings, glutes, lower and upper back, forearms, and upper arms.

A stronger sandbag row means a stronger sandbag everything.

It also acts as a counterbalance to the sandbag box squat. The box squat works the hamstrings a great deal, but it is biased towards the quads. For the health of the knees, and to maintain general athleticism, the hamstrings should never fall behind the quads. The row prevents this potential problem.

The Bear Hug Carry

The bear hug carry is so effective it has its own chapter in the book, but in the context of the *Sandbag Intensity* program I like it for a few reasons.

1. It makes you quick on your feet

The ability to move quickly with heavy weight is something everyone should have. Much of this program is focused on stationary, slower-moving, strength-based exercises. The carry keeps you quick.

2. It improves your ability to breathe with a sandbag held against your chest

Breathing with a sandbag held against the chest is a skill in and of itself, and the bear hug carry is the direct route to improving it. During a set of high-rep box squats a sandbag is held against the chest for many minutes, meaning the bear hug carry has direct carryover.

3. It fills in any gaps in strength you might have

The bear hug carry brings any weak points you might have front and center, and fixes them. If your arms lack the strength to grip a sandbag, they'll be pushed to their limit every set until they adapt. If your bear hug squeezing strength isn't quite there yet, the carry will fix it. If your core is too weak to keep you upright, it will become stronger. The bear hug carry makes you strong everywhere.

Calisthenics

Calisthenics also improves the box squat, while making sure you develop a well-rounded and balanced physique. The core of the *Sandbag Intensity* program may be a squat, but you can expect to grow everywhere.

Pull-ups build the lats, making it easier to keep hold of a sandbag in the bear hug position.

Ab exercises strengthen the core, making you better able to brace when lifting a sandbag.

Pressing exercises build the chest and shoulders, giving you a higher potential for bear hug squeezing strength.

Done in circuit fashion calisthenics builds a lot of muscle in very little time, meaning more resources left over for the box squat.

Calisthenics circuits also improve endurance, further strengthening the cardiovascular system in a way that is very similar to how it works during high-rep box squats.

Circuits also act as a kind of mental refresher. Ultra-high-rep box squats are challenging, but after an intense calisthenics circuit made up of four different exercises, getting to focus on just one movement almost feels like a break.

Isolation

Isolation work is the finishing touch, making sure everything grows, while also directly contributing to the box squat.

Stronger arms means you can keep hold of a sandbag for longer.

The Sandbag-to-Shoulder

You may be wondering about the sandbag-to-shoulder. I spent a lot of time trying to add it to the program, but it never felt right. I believe this was for two reasons.

First, *Sandbag Intensity* is a "put your head down and work" kind of program. It's all about reps, and putting in the effort needed to strengthen the body. It's about showing up to work, getting it done, and getting out.

The sandbag-to-shoulder isn't like that. It falls more in line with Olympic lifting than anything else. It works best when done for relatively low reps with relatively long rest times between those reps. You can't accumulate nearly as much volume with the exercise when lifting heavy weights, and it consumes a lot of resources to do well.

The second reason comes down to focus. The sandbag-to-shoulder is an exercise that typically guides everything else—it's the main event—and it's hard not to get excited about it. I found the more time I spent with the exercise, the less I cared about the box squat. That made it tough to stick with the program.

The sandbag-to-shoulder is great, and I believe improving it is a goal worth working towards, but it wasn't the right fit for this program.

That being said, even if your main goal is becoming better at the sandbag-to-shoulder, I do believe *Sandbag Intensity* is still worth your time. You can think of it as a side quest that offers an insane amount of experience. After a few months with the program, nothing that once challenged you will stand a chance.

Note: I believe the program works best without the sandbag-to-shoulder, but I did find a workaround. See "Chapter Twelve: Alternate Programs" for details.

7

THE SANDBAG BOX SQUAT

Fifty Reps

The core goal of the *Sandbag Intensity* program is taking a weight that challenges you for a set of 10 box squats, and working your way up to a set of 50.

Yes, 50 reps with a 10-rep max.

That may seem an impossible task, and with many exercises it very well might be, but the box squat is special. The secret lies in the bottom position. It's a place of rest. When you're seated on a box with a sandbag on your lap, you can always recover just enough to do another rep. You won't want to. It will be challenging. It will take everything you have to do just one more, but if your mind is strong enough you can keep going.

The only realistic way to squat 50 reps with a 10-rep max is to make use of a technique known as "rest-pause." Rest-pause simply means taking some time between reps to let your muscles recover, so you can continue on doing more reps. The rest you get at the bottom of the sandbag box squat is perfect for this style of training, because you can keep pushing for a very long time without ever letting go of the sandbag.

If you want to squat 50 reps with your 10-rep max, you will eventually reach a point where you'll need upwards of 10–15 seconds rest between every single rep, and that's okay.

These sets are not about speed.

They're not about seeing how many reps you can do in a set time limit.

They're about pushing yourself mind over body to go further, regardless of how long it takes. When you start a set, you need to go in knowing with complete certainty that you will sit on that box all day if that's what's required.

You will hit your rep goal.

It doesn't matter if some outside source says there should be a time limit.

It doesn't matter what anyone else is doing.

This is about tempering the mind to hard work.

The high-rep box squat done in this way is a true test of your dedication. If you don't want it bad enough you will fail. If you have the desire though, you can and will develop a body and mind built for survival.

How To: To perform the sandbag box squat, simply hold a sandbag against your chest with a bear hug grip, sit back onto your box, stand up, and repeat. There are some special techniques you can use when going for ultra-high reps (see 'Chapter Ten: Box Squat Tips' for more information), but the basic form is very straightforward. Don't overthink it.

Note: When performing the box squat, set the box height so you reach parallel or close to it at the bottom of the rep. Your thighs should be roughly parallel to the ground, and the crease of your hips should be at, or slightly below the tops of your knees.

Note: When determining your goal weight for the program, do not rest between reps. That will come later. Pick a weight that challenges you for a set of 10 reps done straight through, without resting on the box between reps.

Weight

For this program you must either have access to multiple sandbags, or have the ability to change the weight of one sandbag. It will not work if you have only one weight. The frequency with that weight will be too high, and progress won't happen in the way we want it to.

At the bare minimum you'll want access to at least three different weights, five is best. This might seem like a lot, and you might not have the space or the resources for five sandbags. That's okay, there's a simple solution to the problem. If owning multiple sandbags isn't an option, instead buy a single adjustable sandbag with a high weight capacity.

1. Fill the sandbag with a base layer of sand.
2. Build 'mini' sandbags out of plastic bags and duct tape, each weighing 5–20 pounds.
3. Add the mini sandbags to the adjustable sandbag as needed.

I recommend your goal sandbag (the sandbag that challenges you for a set of 10 reps initially) be the second heaviest weight you use in the program.

Remember, this starting weight should challenge you for a set of 10 without any extra rest on the box between reps.

Once you have your goal sandbag, decide on the other weights you'll use for the program. Increments of 10–20 pounds work best.

For example, if your goal sandbag weighs 250 pounds, the other weights might be 270, 230, 210, and 190. As I mentioned before, you want your goal weight to be the second heaviest.

190
210
230
250
270

Note: This doesn't need to be set up in perfect increments of 20 pounds, but something along those lines is recommended.

Once you've selected your weights, it's time to get your starting numbers. Choose a different sandbag every workout until you've made it through each one. Typically with the added rest-pause, each set will start somewhere in the 10–30 rep range.

Example:
(Goal sandbag is 250)

Workout One:
250x15

Workout Two:
190x30

Workout Three:
230x20

Workout Four:
210x25

Workout Five:
270x10

Once you have those base numbers, all that's left to do is

come in every workout and try to beat one of your records by five reps.

Note: You may eventually find you can do more than five extra reps, great. Take the opportunity to push further every chance you get. Just make sure you always beat your previous record by at least five reps.

I recommend going by feel. Depending on how the rest of the training day went you will usually feel one weight calling out to you more than the others. There's no need to be strict about this, and I HIGHLY discourage using a set rotation. Choose the weight you'll use in a workout, on the day of that workout based on what sounds exciting.

If that means you only work with your lighter sandbags for a few weeks, that's okay. You'll quickly realize the reps add up fast. Your goal is squatting your 10-rep max for 50, but 50 isn't the cap. With the lighter sandbags you will likely get closer to 100 reps or more. Eventually the thought of pushing your heaviest weight from 15 to 20 will feel like a breeze when compared with taking your lightest from 60 to 65.

Some days you won't even want to look at your heavier weights, and going for high reps with something lighter will appeal to you. This is why I recommend going by feel and not having a set rotation.

8

SANDBAG WORKOUTS

There are two sandbag workouts in the *Sandbag Intensity* program: "Sandbag Workout A" and "Sandbag Workout B."

I recommend you take your time warming up for your sandbag workouts. I personally always do band good mornings and band curls for at least 100–200 reps each before even touching a sandbag. After that I recommend doing at least a few basic lifts from the ground to your lap, and from your lap to your chest using your lightest sandbag. The first exercise of the day is straight into the fire, and you must be prepared.

Both workouts are made up of only three exercises, plus some active recovery at the end. Exercises one and three are the same on both days. The only difference between workouts is exercise two.

Sandbag Workout A
The One-Motion Lift From The Ground To The Chest

The first exercise is the one-motion lift from the ground to the chest, done for five single reps, with 60–90 seconds rest between reps. Choose a weight that challenges you, but lets you lift explosively.

How To: How you do the one-motion lift from the ground to the chest is up to you. You can start with the sandbag lying vertically, horizontally, or standing upright. I recommend choosing whichever lifting style is your go-to preferred method when lifting heavy sandbags.

Note: Always take a deep breath and brace your core before lifting a sandbag.

If you use either of the two basic positions (sandbag lying flat on the ground horizontally or vertically), initiate the movement by first rowing the sandbag to your chest, then forcefully extending your hips until you reach a standing position. The exercise should look something like a row followed by a good morning.

If you prefer starting with the sandbag standing upright, reach down and grab the sandbag with a bear hug grip—holding it tightly against your body—and initiate the movement by simultaneously pressing the ground away with your feet and driving your chest up until you reach a standing position.

The Sandbag Row

Exercise two is the sandbag row done from a horizontal position on the ground.

How To: To perform the exercise, straddle a sandbag and reach your hands under each side, palms facing towards each other. Take a deep breath and brace, and pull the sandbag to your chest while maintaining a horizontal torso angle. Lower the sandbag back down to the ground under control, and repeat for reps.

Weight: Start with a weight that challenges you for an all-out set in the 5–8 rep range.

Reps: When starting out, each set will be submaximal.

If you could do 6 reps in an all-out set while maintaining perfect form, start with 4 reps per set.

If you could do 5, start with 3.

Sets: Once you have your weight and reps per set selected, you'll complete ten sets with 60–90 seconds rest between sets.

Progression: The total number of sets, and the number of reps you do per set will wave over time. This is best explained using an example, but the overarching idea is to start with ten sets, work your way down to five sets, work back up to ten, and repeat.

Example: Let's say you pick 175 pounds for your rowing weight, and you could do an all-out set of 7 reps while maintaining perfect form if you had to.

In workout one you'll do 10 sets of 5 reps with 60–90 seconds rest between sets.

When you repeat the workout, you'll start with one set of 6 reps, followed by eight sets of 5 reps.

Workout three will be two sets of 6 reps, followed by six sets of 5 reps.

For each additional set of 6 you do, the total number of sets will go down by one, until eventually you reach five sets of 6 reps with 60–90 seconds rest between sets.

At that point, you'll begin adding an extra set every workout.

Six sets of 6.

Seven sets of 6.

And so on.

Continue adding an additional set every workout until you reach ten sets of 6 reps. From there you'll repeat the cycle.

One set of 7, eight sets of 6, and so on.

Example:
(Chosen sandbag weight is challenging for an all-out set of 7 reps)

Workout One: 10 sets
(Reps)
5, 5, 5, 5, 5, 5, 5, 5, 5, 5

Workout Two: 9 sets
(Reps)
6, 5, 5, 5, 5, 5, 5, 5, 5

Workout Three: 8 sets
(Reps)
6, 6, 5, 5, 5, 5, 5, 5

Workout Four: 7 sets
(Reps)
6, 6, 6, 5, 5, 5, 5

Workout Five: 6 sets
(Reps)
6, 6, 6, 6, 5, 5

Workout Six: 5 sets
(Reps)
6, 6, 6, 6, 6

Workout Seven: 6 sets
(Reps)
6, 6, 6, 6, 6, 6

Workout Eight: 7 sets
(Reps)
6, 6, 6, 6, 6, 6, 6

Workout Nine: 8 sets
(Reps)
6, 6, 6, 6, 6, 6, 6, 6

Workout Ten: 9 sets
(Reps)
6, 6, 6, 6, 6, 6, 6, 6, 6

Workout Eleven: 10 sets
(Reps)
6, 6, 6, 6, 6, 6, 6, 6, 6, 6

Workout Twelve: 9 sets
(Reps)
7, 6, 6, 6, 6, 6, 6, 6, 6

And so on.

I recommend capping the volume at ten sets of 8 reps. Once you reach that point, add weight and start over.

You can also increase the weight sooner if you'd like. This comes down to personal preference. If you manage ten sets of 7 reps with 175 pounds for example, you might move to a 200 pound sandbag and start over, rather than taking 175 all the way to ten sets of 8.

Note: Resist the temptation to jump ahead early. Trust the process. Over time this slow and steady progression model will make you significantly stronger.

Note: Strive for perfect form at all times. Try your best to maintain a flat back position, and drive with your legs as hard as you can. Keep in mind the sandbag row is as much about the hamstrings as it is about the back.

Note: Sandbag rows demand a lot from your arms. For this reason, I highly recommend spending your rest time between sets doing high-rep curls with a light band. Pump away 50–100 reps between every set, rotating between underhand, neutral, and overhand curling positions. The extra blood flow will go a long way towards keeping your muscles and tendons healthy.

The Sandbag Box Squat

After rows it's time for the main event, the sandbag box squat. Choose your weight for the day, sit down on the box, and don't stop squatting until you beat your previous record by at least five reps. As stated earlier, time is not a variable here. Just keep going until you're done.

You must not fail to get your reps! The entire program depends on you succeeding here.

Posterior Chain & Abs

After squats one step remains, direct work for the posterior chain and abs.

This part is essential, don't skip it.

Not only will this direct work increase your strength and muscle size, but it also acts as a form of active recovery.

You will need it.

For the posterior chain, choose either band good mornings with a relatively light band (something you could rep out for at least 30–40 reps in a set if you had to), or some kind of body-weight back extension. I personally favor the 45-degree hyperextension, but any variation will do.

Once you have your exercise, do 100 reps.

I like splitting this up into sets of 30, 25, 20, 15, and 10, but any rep scheme will do.

4x25.

34, 33, 33.

Just do 100 reps.

This should not be intense, or even remotely challenging when compared with the rest of the workout. This is about pumping blood into the muscles, not causing muscle damage.

After the posterior chain exercise, choose a basic bodyweight ab exercise (crunches, sit-ups, flutter kicks, leg lifts, etc.) and do 100 reps.

Finish with 50 oblique crunches per side and call it a day.

Note: Yes, there are more efficient methods out there for working the abs. Those methods also require more effort, and you will not have any extra effort to spare when running this program. High-rep sets get the job done without wearing you down any more than you already are.

Working the abs in this way also has direct carryover to the sandbag box squat. High-rep training conditions the abs to keep going for a long time, which is exactly what you'll need to push your box squats to the extreme.

Sandbag Workout B
The One-Motion Lift From The Ground To The Chest

As with "Sandbag Workout A," begin today's workout with 5 powerful one-motion lifts from the ground to the chest with 60–90 seconds rest between reps.

Note: There's no need to rotate through each of the three different starting positions (horizontal, vertical, and standing upright), just use whichever position you prefer.

The Bear Hug Carry

Exercise two is the bear hug carry.

How To: To perform the exercise, hold a sandbag against your chest with a bear hug grip, and start walking.

Weight: Choose a weight you could carry for somewhere in the 30–40 second range, and do your sets for 10 seconds less than that.

Example: If you could carry a weight for an all-out set of 30 seconds, start with 20 seconds per set.

Progression: Once you have your weight and distance selected, follow the same setup used for rows in "Sandbag Workout A": 10 sets with 60–90 seconds rest between sets, working from 10 sets down to 5, and back up again.

Note: Taking a heavy bear hug carry to complete failure is extremely mentally fatiguing. It's unlikely anyone could manage it ten times in a single workout, let alone follow that up with an all-out set of box squats. For this reason, your starting sets will be done for 10 seconds less than your max, and you'll move up in increments of only 5 seconds every workout.

Example:
(Chosen sandbag weight is challenging for an all-out set of 30 seconds)

Workout One: 10 sets
(Seconds)
20, 20, 20, 20, 20, 20, 20, 20, 20, 20

Workout Two: 9 sets
(Seconds)
25, 20, 20, 20, 20, 20, 20, 20, 20

Workout Three: 8 sets
(Seconds)
25, 25, 20, 20, 20, 20, 20, 20

Workout Four: 7 sets
(Seconds)
25, 25, 25, 20, 20, 20, 20

Workout Five: 6 sets
(Seconds)
25, 25, 25, 25, 20, 20

Workout Six: 5 sets
(Seconds)
25, 25, 25, 25, 25

Workout Seven: 6 sets
(Seconds)
25, 25, 25, 25, 25, 25

Workout Eight: 7 sets
(Seconds)
25, 25, 25, 25, 25, 25, 25

Workout Nine: 8 sets
(Seconds)
25, 25, 25, 25, 25, 25, 25, 25

Workout Ten: 9 sets
(Seconds)
25, 25, 25, 25, 25, 25, 25, 25

Workout Eleven: 10 sets
(Seconds)
25, 25, 25, 25, 25, 25, 25, 25

Workout Twelve: 9 sets
(Seconds)
30, 25, 25, 25, 25, 25, 25, 25, 25

And so on.

I recommend capping this at ten sets of 40 seconds maximum, otherwise the volume becomes too much, and the effort level becomes too high. Stay within the 20–40 second range if possible.

Note: If you have access to some kind of platform, place your sandbag on it between sets. The lift from the ground was worked earlier in the day, and was strengthened during "Sandbag Workout A" with rows. All that matters here is the carry.

Note: I highly recommend spending your rest time between sets doing high-rep curls with a light band. Pump away 50–100 reps between every set, rotating between underhand, neutral, and overhand curling positions. The extra blood flow will go a long way towards keeping your muscles and tendons healthy.

The Sandbag Box Squat

After carries, it's time once again for the all-out set of box squats. Choose your weight, settle in, and beat your previous record by at least five reps.

Posterior Chain & Abs

Finish the workout with direct work for the posterior chain and abs, and call it a day.

Deload
Take a full week off from training at the end of every row and bear hug carry cycle.

Example:
10 sets
9 sets
8 sets
7 sets
6 sets
5 sets
6 sets
7 sets
8 sets
9 sets
Deload Week
10 sets
9 sets

And so on.

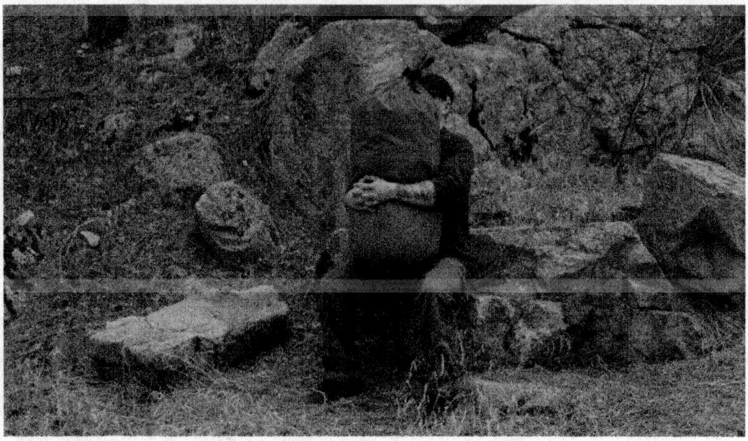

9

CALISTHENICS WORKOUTS

The calisthenics part of the program will be done using high-intensity circuits.

Ladders

There are many different options available for setting up a calisthenics circuit, but with *Sandbag Intensity*—a strength-endurance program focused on the sandbag box squat—I've found shorter circuits work best.

My recommendation for this program is using four exercises, and keeping your circuits in the 20-25 minute range.

Note: For best results and complete muscular development everywhere, I recommend using one of the following setups:

Exercise 1: Vertical Pull
Exercise 2: Horizontal Push
Exercise 3: Ab Exercise
Exercise 4: Vertical Push

Or

Exercise 1: Vertical Pull
Exercise 2: Vertical Push
Exercise 3: Ab Exercise
Exercise 4: Horizontal Push

Note: 20–25 minutes is short enough to allow for continuous high-intensity work, letting you sufficiently stimulate your muscles and cardiovascular system without pushing the volume unnecessarily high.

A quick circuit like this also allows for more time spent on isolation work, another vital part of the program.

Because the window of time is so small, long continuous circuit setups like a "10 down" are nearly impossible to manage. For this reason, I recommend using ladders and going for rounds.

Rather than a "10 down," you'll instead use something like a 6-5-4 or a 5-3-2 setup.

Note: Ladders make it easy to continue adding work over time, while staying within the 20–25 minute time frame.

Using the 5-3-2 ladder as an example (5 reps of each exercise, 3 reps of each exercise, 2 reps of each exercise), all you have to do is complete the ladder as many times as you can within the 20–25 minute window. If you complete the ladder three times in 24 minutes the first time you attempt it, come back next workout and try to complete it three times in 23 minutes and 59 seconds or less. From there you'll continue working with the circuit until you reach 20 minutes, at which point you'll add another round and start over.

Example Circuit:
Pull-ups, Dips, Hanging Leg Raises, Pike Push-ups
5-3-2 Ladder

Workout One:
5 Pull-ups
5 Dips
5 Hanging Leg Raises
5 Pike Push-ups
3 Pull-ups
3 Dips
3 Hanging Leg Raises
3 Pike Push-ups
2 Pull-ups
2 Dips
2 Hanging Leg Raises
2 Pike Push-ups

5 Pull-ups
5 Dips
5 Hanging Leg Raises
5 Pike Push-ups
3 Pull-ups
3 Dips
3 Hanging Leg Raises
3 Pike Push-ups
2 Pull-ups
2 Dips
2 Hanging Leg Raises
2 Pike Push-ups

5 Pull-ups
5 Dips
5 Hanging Leg Raises
5 Pike Push-ups
3 Pull-ups
3 Dips

3 Hanging Leg Raises
3 Pike Push-ups
2 Pull-ups
2 Dips
2 Hanging Leg Raises
2 Pike Push-ups

Time: 21 Minutes and 30 Seconds

The ladder was completed three times, and took 21 minutes and 30 seconds. Perfect. In this example you would continue attempting the exact same circuit until you complete it in 20 minutes or less, at which point you would add another round.

Example:
Workout One: 3 Rounds
21 Minutes and 30 Seconds

Workout Two: 3 Rounds
20 Minutes and 50 Seconds

Workout Three: 3 Rounds
20 Minutes and 35 Seconds

Workout Four: 3 Rounds
20 Minutes and 30 Seconds

Workout Five: 3 Rounds
20 Minutes and 28 Seconds

Workout Six: 3 Rounds
20 Minutes and 22 Seconds

Workout Seven: 3 Rounds
20 Minutes and 19 Seconds

Workout Eight: 3 Rounds
20 Minutes and 15 Seconds

Workout Nine: 3 Rounds
20 Minutes and 9 Seconds

Workout Ten: 3 Rounds
20 Minutes and 5 Seconds

Workout Eleven: 3 Rounds
19 Minutes and 59 Seconds

The circuit was completed in under 20 minutes, time to add another round. Next workout, complete the ladder four times through, record your time, and continue on.

Workout Twelve: 4 Rounds
23 Minutes and 20 Seconds

Workout Thirteen: 4 Rounds
23 Minutes and 11 Seconds

And so on.

Exercise Selection

When setting up a circuit, exercise selection is extremely important. Always remember the calisthenics circuits in this book are meant to develop muscle and endurance at the same time. The goal is achieving complete balance between the two, so you get both in equal parts.

How far can you push a muscle without needing to slow down or rest?

What's the exact perfect difficulty level for each exercise that allows you to get close to failure in the muscles, while maintaining a steady pace and challenging your endurance?

Without proper planning one thing will overpower the other.

If the exercises you choose are too easy, you'll end up too winded to push your muscles near failure.

If the exercises are too difficult, the muscles will wear out long before your endurance is challenged.

Achieving balance might take some work, but the rewards are well worth it.

If the circuits shown in the *Sandbag Intensity* program aren't working for you, change them. No one circuit is better than any other.

Here are a few things to look for when first attempting a circuit:

1. **Were you so out of breath you couldn't push your muscles to their limit?**

If this is an issue for you, my recommendation is switching to exercise variations with a higher difficulty level, and reducing the number of reps you do per set.

For example, if a basic 6-5-4 circuit made up of pull-ups, diamond push-ups, hanging leg raises, and pike push-ups was too difficult on the endurance side of things, you might switch to a 5-3-2 circuit, and do chest-to-bar pull-ups, decline diamond push-ups, hanging leg raises, and decline pike push-ups.

Note: Fewer total reps means less total movement, and less movement means less of an endurance challenge. Switching to exercise variations with a higher difficulty level lets you push your muscles to failure with fewer reps.

2. Were the exercises too difficult, preventing you from moving fast enough to sufficiently challenge your endurance?

This usually means you should switch to easier exercise variations, and use higher reps.

For example, if a 5-3-2 circuit made up of pull-ups, dips, ab wheel rollouts, and decline pike push-ups is causing you trouble, you might switch to a 6-5-4 circuit and do inverted rows, diamond push-ups, ab wheel rollouts, and pike push-ups.

Note: With easier exercises, you'll need more total reps to push your muscles to failure. More reps means more movement and a greater endurance challenge.

Note: Although pull-ups and inverted rows represent different movement patterns (pull-ups are a vertical pull, and inverted rows are a horizontal pull), they're both still 'pulling' exercises. Maintaining balance between push and pull is more important than sticking to one specific movement pattern. Always feel free to switch from one pattern to another if necessary.

3. Was one exercise at a much higher difficulty level than the rest?

This is the problem you're most likely to encounter. Typically it's either the pull-up variation, or the pike push-up variation that causes the issue. To fix the problem, simply reduce the difficulty of the most difficult exercise.

If standard pull-ups are holding you back, consider switching to an easier variation, using band assistance, or doing inverted rows instead.

If decline pike push-ups are too difficult for you, consider switching to standard pike push-ups on the floor, pike push-ups with bent knees, or instead doing a hybrid movement like Hindu push-ups.

Note: Always remember the goal with these circuits is maintaining a steady pace. If one exercise is too difficult and slows you down, the circuit won't work as intended.

4. **Was one exercise significantly easier than the rest?**

This is also a simple fix. If one exercise feels too easy compared to the rest, increase the difficulty. If a push-up variation is too easy, consider elevating your feet. If pull-ups are too easy, switch to chest-to-bar pull-ups, use a wide grip, or work with a more challenging variation like sternum pull-ups.

Note: The goal is balancing muscle and endurance. If the exercises you choose are too easy, a circuit probably won't build much muscle.

There are countless ways to set up a calisthenics circuit. Find something that challenges you as an individual, and you will see results.

Isolation Work

After the calisthenics circuit training, it's time for some isolation work.

Neck

For the neck, you'll do four sets of 25 neck curls and neck extensions, alternating back and forth between each (that's four sets of neck curls and four sets of neck extensions). This includes warm-up sets. Each set should be progressively heavier. There is no need to rest between sets.

Arms & Shoulders

Direct isolation work for the arms and shoulders is made up of three parts:

1. One set for each of the six forearm movements (flexion, extension, supination, pronation, radial deviation, and ulnar deviation).

The goal is reaching muscular failure in the 10–30 rep range for each exercise.

Flexion: Wrist curls

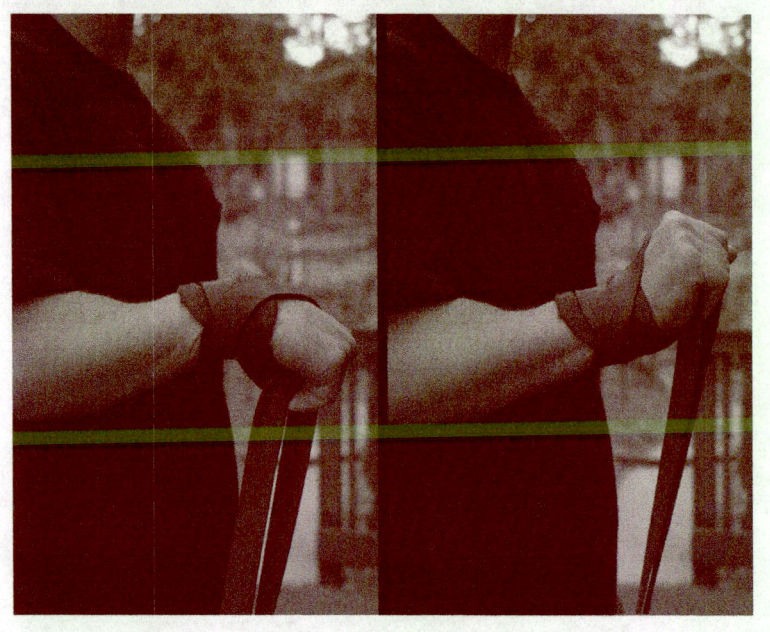

Extension: Reverse wrist curls

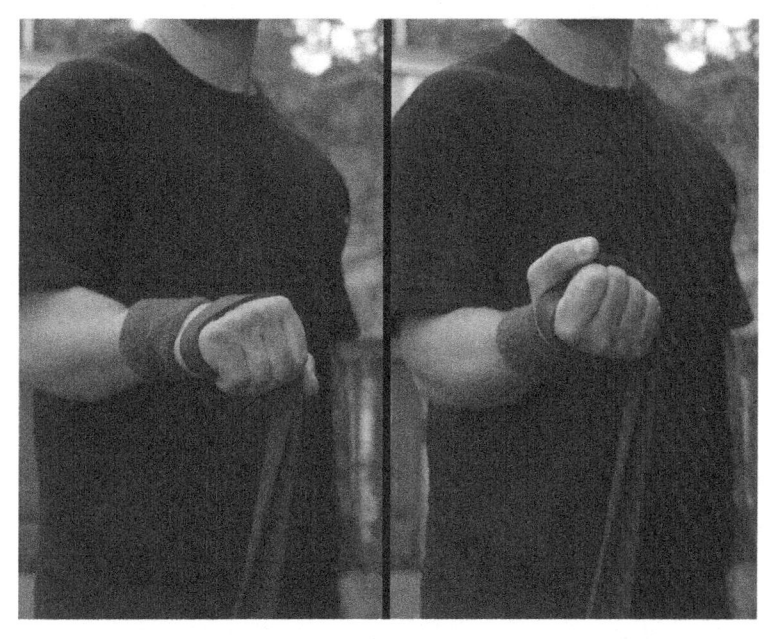

Supination: *Start with your palms facing down, and move to a palms facing up position*

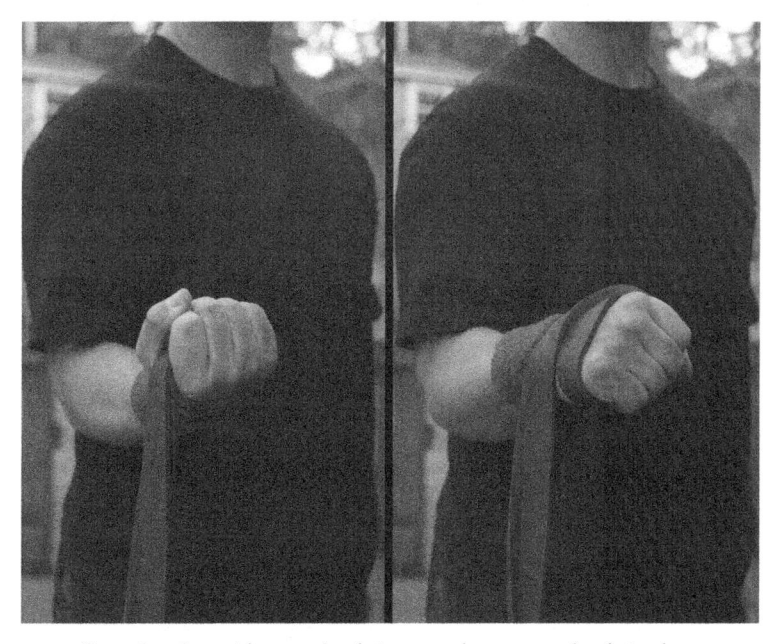

Pronation: *Start with your palms facing up, and move to a palms facing down position*

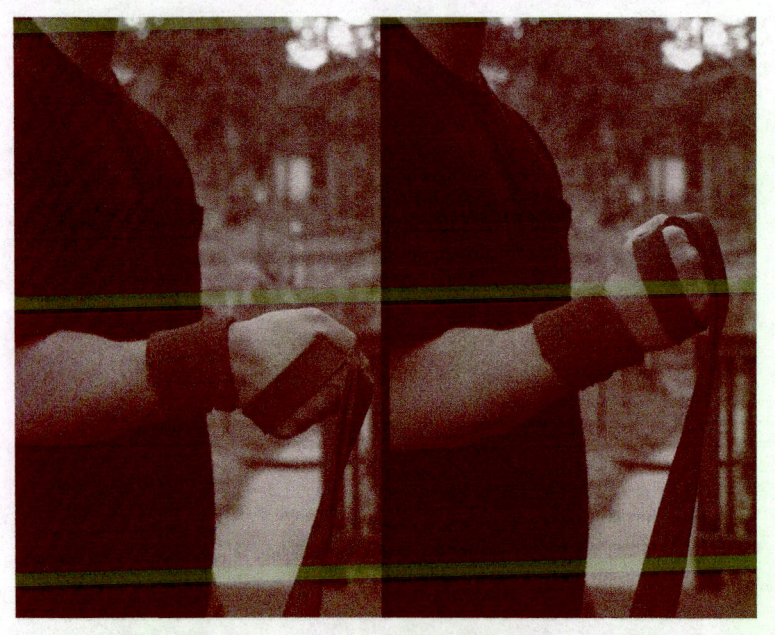

Radial Deviation: *Start with your hand in a neutral position, and raise your fist up towards the sky*

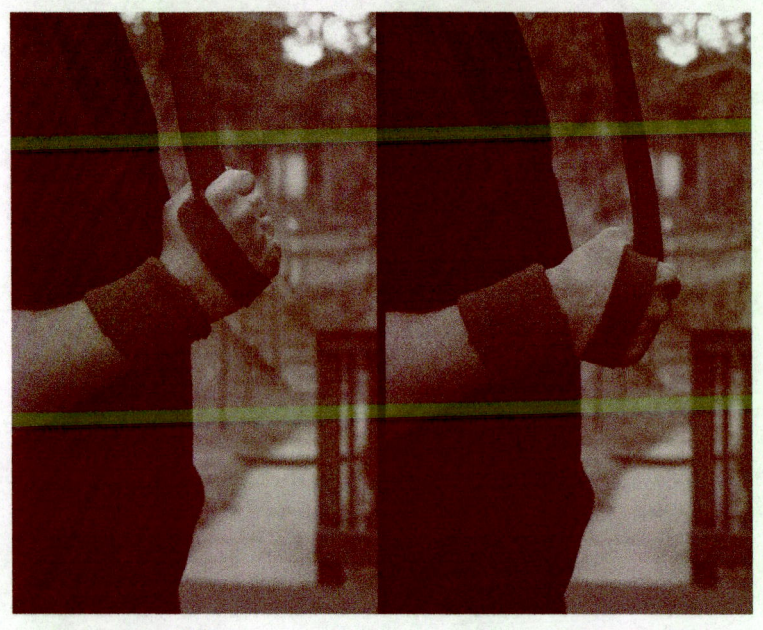

Ulnar Deviation: *Start with your hand in a neutral position, and lower your fist down towards the ground*

Note: I realize recommending an exercise for each of the six forearm movements might seem unnecessary—that's a lot of work for such a small area—but you'll have to trust me on this one. Most lifters have a LOT of untapped potential here. If you've been neglecting any one of these movements, you have some serious gains waiting for you. Enjoy.

Directly targeting each of these movements also has some very positive effects on the health of the wrists and elbows.

Note: When I ran the program, I used resistance bands to work each of these movements separately. If you don't have time for that, rice bucket training or leveraging a steel mace are great alternatives.

Note: If you're very short on time you can skip most of this. At the very least I recommend doing wrist curls and wrist extensions.

2. Giant set: bicep curls, tricep extensions, and a shoulder exercise done for two sets each.

The goal is reaching muscular failure in the 10–30 rep range for each exercise.

Do a set of bicep curls, then a set of tricep extensions, and finish with a set for the shoulders. Move from one exercise to the next without resting between sets.

After you've made it through each exercise once, rest for 2–3 minutes, and repeat the giant set a second time.

Note: For the shoulders I recommend pull-aparts or face pulls. These exercises work both the rear and side delts at the same time, and are great for posture. If you can't do either of these, side lateral raises are another great option.

3. Tricep pushdowns done for one set of 100 reps

Complete one long rest-pause set of 100 reps with a weight you could ordinarily do for a hard set of 30–50.

Note: Progression won't always happen every workout, but do your best to bring some intensity to your isolation work. Try to increase reps and/or weight over time.

Isolation Exercises

When I ran the program I trained my neck with a band-loaded head harness, and my arms/shoulders with a chest expander and resistance bands. I mention this for transparency, but the exact equipment you use isn't important. There are countless tools that will get the job done, just use whatever you have available. As long as you follow the basic guidelines you will see results.

It would be highly unnecessary for me to list every possible option for every exercise, so I'll leave this part up to personal preference.

For example, one of the exercises is a curl. Long drawn out lists detailing which curl is best makes for good fitness content, but at the end of the day a curl is a curl. Don't stress about it. If you have dumbbells available, use dumbbell curls in the program. If you have a barbell, use that. Machines, bands, a chest expander, gymnastics rings, kettlebells, a backpack filled with weight—all of these things work.

For the forearm exercises a band is effective, but most tools can be manipulated to work the forearms in a similar way.

The same is true for each movement.

Pick an exercise you like, force yourself to become stronger with that exercise over time, and you will grow.

In case you're interested, here are the exact exercises I used myself when running the program:

Forearms: Each movement done with heavy band tension
Bicep Curls: Chest expander curls
Tricep Extensions: Chest expander sideways extensions
Shoulder Exercise: Chest expander pull-aparts
Tricep Pushdowns: A heavy band attached to my pull-up bar

10

BOX SQUAT TIPS

One: The Box

Use a box height that gets you close to parallel at the bottom of the rep. When sitting on the box your thighs should be roughly parallel to the ground, and the crease of your hips should be at roughly the same height, or slightly below the tops of your knees.

If the box is too low your legs will face a much greater challenge, and you'll be limited on how much weight you can use. This means less of a stimulus for the muscles of the back.

Set too high and the legs won't be nearly as involved. The added weight you'll need to use to compensate for the smaller range of motion also means more fatigue, and managing recovery will become much more challenging.

A parallel position is the perfect balance of weight and range of motion, evenly stimulating the most amount of muscle, and letting you push your sets furthest.

Two: Clothing

The clothing you wear can have a huge impact on your sets. If you wear pants made of a slick material, you'll have trouble keeping hold of the sandbag in the bottom position, making that position less a place of rest and more like a constant battle against the sandbag falling between your legs. If you wear a slick shirt, keeping a solid grip on the sandbag as you stand up will become much more challenging, and will only hold you back.

Don't put yourself at an unnecessary disadvantage. Doing your box squats with slick clothing would be like doing a heavy farmer's carry without straps. Sure your grip would be challenged, but the rest of your body would never get even remotely close to failure.

Course material or direct skin contact makes for the best grip, and a better chance at reaching high reps. If you wear a shirt, I recommend short sleeves or a tank top for the extra friction you'll gain between your arms and the sandbag. The shirt should ideally be made from some kind of rough-spun cotton or canvas material. For the ultimate grip you might consider forgoing a shirt altogether if that's a possibility. The same is true with pants. Short shorts are an option, thick cotton sweatpants or canvas/denim work pants are too if they allow you the proper mobility.

Three: Music and Emotion

This comes down to personal preference (not all music does the same thing for everyone), but you'll want to avoid listening to music that gets you overly amped up. These high-rep sets are not the same as a typical set of ten or a one-rep max, and you cannot approach them in the same way. Rather than getting fired up and attacking the weight, it's better to ease your way into the set. Accept that no amount of preparation for what you're about to attempt will ever be enough. Starting overly aggressive will only wear you down faster.

Four: The Platform

If you have access to some kind of platform, I highly recommend placing your sandbag on it before you begin your set. Lifting a heavy sandbag from the ground at the start of the set adds unnecessary fatigue. It may also force you to tap into a state of mind you don't want to be in. As I mentioned in the previous segment on music and emotion, starting overly aggressive will cause you to wear out much faster. If a sandbag is heavy enough, you'll have no choice but to bring the aggression to lift it off the ground, setting you up to fail from the start.

Placing the sandbag on a platform also gives you the opportunity to make sure it isn't too out of shape at the beginning of the set. Lifting a sandbag from the ground often causes the sand to shift out of place, and from the platform you can shift it back into the position you want.

This might not seem like a big deal, but it is. These sets can go on for a very long time, and a small inconvenience spread out over many minutes is likely to become a huge factor.

Five: Grip and Chalk

It's a good idea to completely coat your hands in chalk before the set. I apply it to my palms and the backs of my hands. This helps with grip initially, and can give you an edge.

That said, if you're someone who's typically a bit over reliant on chalk you will need to get used to going without. Usually somewhere around rep 20 your hands will become sweaty and the chalk will disappear, meaning you'll need to switch tactics.

My preferred method is starting the set with chalk and a fingers interlocked grip. This is a passive grip, relying as much on friction as it does strength. Starting with this grip lets you conserve energy for later. Once the chalk disappears I'll switch to an S grip. The S grip is taken from grappling sports and is very strong, even when your hands are sweaty. It does take more effort though, which is why I prefer starting with the fingers interlocked grip.

Once I switch to the S grip, I'll change positions every five reps or so, moving the outside hand to the inside and vice versa. This helps with managing fatigue, and makes sure one arm doesn't wear out before the other.

Six: Stance

You may need to narrow your stance to prevent the sandbag from falling between your legs when seated on the box. If your sandbag is wide enough to allow for it, you might consider changing stance width as you move through the set. This changes the stimulus placed on the legs and will give you a slight advantage.

Seven: Where to Grip the Sandbag

For best results, grip the sandbag somewhere between the middle and three-quarters of the way up.

Gripping the very top of the sandbag may initially seem like the easier option, and for the first few reps it might be, but you'll be setting yourself up for failure later on. As you move through the set the sandbag will change its shape, and the sand will become tightly packed above and below where your arms are. If you grip too high all of the sand will end up below your arms, meaning at a certain point you'll actually need to grip very low on the sandbag to keep hold of it, making things significantly more challenging.

If you grab too low on the sandbag from the start, your upper body will have to work much harder to lift it on every rep, and you might find your lower back wears out long before your legs do. Gripping somewhere between halfway and three-quarters of the way up is the sweet spot. The sand will end up tightly packed below your arms, but a good amount will remain above your arms too, making for an easier time gripping the sandbag.

Eight: Rocking

These high-rep box squats are not about targeting any one muscle over another, they're about moving the weight. Forcing yourself to lift without momentum is unnecessary, and will only hold you back. Initiate every rep by creating as much momentum as you can. Start by rocking backward, then reversing the motion to propel yourself off the box.

Rather than some kind of cheap trick, this actually allows your body to fatigue evenly. If you do every rep without momentum, your legs will wear out long before your upper body does. Rocking on the box causes these things to fatigue at an even pace. The sandbag box squat is not a 'legs' exercise; it's a full-body movement.

I also recommend rocking back and forth during your rest time while seated on the box. Not only will this help you to enter a kind of trance where the constant movement all blends together into one continuous thing, but rocking also keeps the sandbag from resting in any one position for too long. While the bottom position is a place of rest, eventually you will start to feel the weight of the sandbag resting on your thighs. Constant movement prevents any one spot from becoming overly burdened.

Nine: Bracing

You will eventually reach a point in the set where the idea of bracing your core with the valsalva maneuver seems like an impossible task.

You must not give in.

Even though the reps are high, this is still heavy lifting.

Doing heavy reps without properly bracing is asking for trouble.

I learned this lesson the hard way and ended up with a sore lower back for days after doing a set of 100 without any real bracing after rep 50.

Brace your core before every single rep.

Note: Bracing your core does not mean holding your breath. Holding your breath for 50 reps is a recipe for a terrible tension headache. As you lift, release some air by grunting, growling, or making a "tss" sound. Fully breathe out at the top of the rep and reset before lowering back down to the box.

Ten: Full Range of Motion

A full range of motion leads to maximum gains and lets you push your sets further than you could with a partial range of motion. Always stand all the way up. Fully extend your hips and flex your glutes at the top of every rep. Keep the sandbag held tightly against your chest at all times. Do not allow it to sag down towards your waist.

Eleven: Rep Count

If you're going for a set of 60 reps, the last thing you want to do is count in your head all the way to 60. Instead I recommend splitting the reps into two or three parts. Rather than 60, count to 30, start over at zero, and count to 30 again.

You can also change tactics partway through.

I'll often go into a set with the intention of counting to 30 twice, then split the second set of 30 into multiple parts.

30 + 30 = 60 reps
30 + 20 + 10 = 60 reps
30 + 20 + 5 + 3 + 2 = 60 reps

The reps are the same either way, but doing this almost feels like a break, like you're letting yourself off easy—and that can make a big difference.

If you plan on splitting a set into two parts, you might also consider making the first part longer.

For example, if I'm going for 60 reps I'll often think of the set as 40 + 20. After 40 reps, a set of 20 feels like nothing.

You can combine this with the first idea too:

40 + 20 = 60 reps
40 + 10 + 10 = 60 reps
40 + 10 + 5 + 3 + 2 = 60 reps

You might also consider pushing the first part of a set further than planned.

If the original plan was 40 + 20 for example, you might instead push that first part all the way to 45.

This method works on the basic idea of delayed gratification. Finishing the first part of a set feels like an accomplishment, and by pushing that accomplishment further out, the set ends up feeling like less of a challenge in the end.

This is my favorite technique. After a few months with these high-rep sets, I came to live for that 'in-between' place. That space between where you originally planned on resetting back at zero, and where you actually do.

Example: If the goal is 40 + 20 but I do 50 + 10 instead, reps 41-50 are always the best. Every single one of them always leaves me with the feeling that I'm somehow getting away with something.

Using these techniques, you might find you reach your

target rep goal and realize another five reps wouldn't actually be so bad. When that happens, go for the extra reps! Don't worry that more reps today means even more reps next time. If you can do it once, you can do it again.

Twelve: Time Limit

There is no time limit when doing these sets.

The time is irrelevant.

Tell yourself at the start of the set that you will sit on that box all day if you have to.

You will get those reps.

Take as many deep breaths as you need while seated on the box.

The goal is not condensing the set to fit within an arbitrary time limit. The goal is and always will be doing more than last time, regardless of how long it takes.

These extreme sets are all mind over body.

Your body will recover enough for another rep, you just need to make yourself do it.

For reference, as I approached my goal of squatting 50 reps with my 10-rep max, my average time per rep was typically in the 8–12 second range. Don't worry about the time, just keep going.

Thirteen: Stretch Out the Arms and Legs

Stretch out your arms and legs as needed. After 5 minutes your legs will probably start to cramp, and depending on the grip you use, your arms will feel an intense burn. Shift the sandbag onto one leg and extend the other for a second, then repeat on the opposite side.

Take one arm away from the sandbag and reach it behind you, then repeat with the other.

You may eventually reach the point where you need to do this between every single rep, and that's okay.

11

SANDBAG INTENSITY

The Sandbag Intensity Program

Monday: Sandbag Workout A

1. **Sandbag One-Motion Lift From The Ground To The Chest**
   - 5 single reps with 60–90 seconds rest between reps
2. **Sandbag Row**
   - 5–10 sets with 60–90 seconds rest between sets
3. **Sandbag Box Squat**
   - 1 set
4. **Posterior Chain**
   - 100 reps
5. **Abs**
   - 100 reps
6. **Obliques**
   - 50 reps per side

Tuesday: Calisthenics Workout A

1. **Calisthenics Circuit:**
   - Neutral Pull-ups, Diamond Push-ups, Ab Wheel Rollouts (or hanging leg raises), Pike Push-ups
   - Rep Scheme: 6-5-4 done for rounds (20–25 minute range)
2. **Neck:**
   - Neck Curls + Neck Extensions
   - 4 sets of 25 reps each
3. **Forearms:**
   - Flexion Movement
   - Extension Movement
   - Supination Movement
   - Pronation Movement
   - Radial Deviation Movement
   - Ulnar Deviation Movement
   - 1 set to failure each in the 10–30 rep range
4. **Arms/Shoulders**
   - Bicep Curl + Tricep Extension + Shoulder Exercise
   - 2 sets to failure each in the 10–30 rep range
5. **Tricep Pushdowns**
   - 1 set of 100 reps

Wednesday: Off

Thursday: Sandbag Workout B

1. **Sandbag One-Motion Lift From The Ground To The Chest**
   - 5 single reps with 60–90 seconds rest between reps
2. **Sandbag Bear Hug Carry**
   - 5–10 sets with 60–90 seconds rest between sets
3. **Sandbag Box Squat**
   - 1 set
4. **Posterior Chain**
   - 100 reps
5. **Abs**
   - 100 reps
6. **Obliques**
   - 50 reps per side

Friday: Calisthenics Workout B

1. **Calisthenics Circuit:**
   - Pull-ups, Dips, Hanging Leg Raises, Decline Pike Push-ups
   - Rep Scheme: 5-3-2 done for rounds (20–25 minute range)
2. **Neck:**
   - Neck Curls + Neck Extensions
   - 4 sets of 25 reps each
3. **Forearms:**
   - Flexion Movement
   - Extension Movement
   - Supination Movement
   - Pronation Movement

- Radial Deviation Movement
- Ulnar Deviation Movement
- 1 set to failure each in the 10–30 rep range
4. **Arms/Shoulders**
    - Bicep Curl + Tricep Extension + Shoulder Exercise
    - 2 sets to failure each in the 10–30 rep range
5. **Tricep Pushdowns**
    - 1 set of 100 reps

Saturday: Off

Sunday: Sandbag Workout A

Monday: Calisthenics Workout A

Tuesday: Off

Wednesday: Sandbag Workout B

And so on.

12

ALTERNATE PROGRAMS

I Need To Train On The Same Days Every Week

Monday: Sandbag Workout A

1. **Sandbag One-Motion Lift From The Ground To The Chest**
    - 5 single reps with 60–90 seconds rest between reps
2. **Sandbag Row**
    - 5–10 sets with 60–90 seconds rest between sets
3. **Sandbag Box Squat**
    - 1 set
4. **Posterior Chain**
    - 100 reps
5. **Abs**
    - 100 reps
6. **Obliques**
    - 50 reps per side

Tuesday: Calisthenics Workout A

1. **Calisthenics Circuit:**
     - Neutral Pull-ups, Diamond Push-ups, Ab Wheel Rollouts (or hanging leg raises), Pike Push-ups
     - Rep Scheme: 6-5-4 done for rounds (20–25 minute range)
2. **Neck:**
     - Neck Curls + Neck Extensions
     - 4 sets of 25 reps each
3. **Forearms:**
     - Flexion Movement
     - Extension Movement
     - Supination Movement
     - Pronation Movement
     - Radial Deviation Movement
     - Ulnar Deviation Movement
     - 1 set to failure each in the 10–30 rep range
4. **Arms/Shoulders**
     - Bicep Curl + Tricep Extension + Shoulder Exercise
     - 2 sets to failure each in the 10–30 rep range
5. **Tricep Pushdowns**
     - 1 set of 100 reps

Wednesday: Off

Thursday: Sandbag Workout B

1. **Sandbag One-Motion Lift From The Ground To The Chest**
   - 5 single reps with 60–90 seconds rest between reps
2. **Sandbag Bear Hug Carry**
   - 5–10 sets with 60–90 seconds rest between sets
3. **Sandbag Box Squat**
   - 1 set
4. **Posterior Chain**
   - 100 reps
5. **Abs**
   - 100 reps
6. **Obliques**
   - 50 reps per side

Friday: Calisthenics Workout B

1. **Calisthenics Circuit:**
   - Pull-ups, Dips, Hanging Leg Raises, Decline Pike Push-ups
   - Rep Scheme: 5-3-2 done for rounds (20–25 minute range)
2. **Neck:**
   - Neck Curls + Neck Extensions
   - 4 sets of 25 reps each
3. **Forearms:**
   - Flexion Movement
   - Extension Movement
   - Supination Movement

- Pronation Movement
- Radial Deviation Movement
- Ulnar Deviation Movement
- 1 set to failure each in the 10–30 rep range
4. **Arms/Shoulders**
   - Bicep Curl + Tricep Extension + Shoulder Exercise
   - 2 sets to failure each in the 10–30 rep range
5. **Tricep Pushdowns**
   - 1 set of 100 reps

Saturday: Off

Sunday: Off

Repeat.

I Can't Go Without The Sandbag-To-Shoulder

I believe the program works best as is, but I did find a workaround for anyone who doesn't want to go months without practicing the sandbag-to-shoulder. For this variation of the program we'll add an extra sandbag day to the rotation.

Sandbag Workout A.
Sandbag Workout B.
Sandbag Workout C.

Workout C uses the sandbag shoulder carry as its second exercise. The shoulder carry combines the sandbag-to-shoulder with the "put your head down and work" attitude of the program.

Workout C begins the same as workouts A and B with the one-motion lift from the ground to the chest, done for 5 single reps with 60–90 seconds rest between reps.

Exercise two is the sandbag shoulder carry, done for five sets of 20–40 seconds per shoulder (that's ten sets total).

How To: To perform the sandbag shoulder carry, simply lift a sandbag to your shoulder, keep hold of it with both hands, and start walking.

Note: Unlike the row and the bear hug carry, the total number of sets for this exercise will not change over time. This is done to keep practice volume high.

Weight: Choose a weight you could carry for an all-out set in the 30–40 second range, and do your sets for 10 seconds less than that.

Example/Progression: If you can carry a weight for 30 seconds, go for 20 seconds every set.

Every workout replace one set of 20 seconds per shoulder with a set of 25 seconds per shoulder.

Example:

Workout One: Five sets of 20 seconds per shoulder.

Workout Two: One set of 25 seconds per shoulder. Four sets of 20 seconds per shoulder.

Workout Three: Two sets of 25 seconds per shoulder. Three sets of 20 seconds per shoulder.

Workout Four: Three sets of 25 seconds per shoulder. Two sets of 20 seconds per shoulder.

Workout Five: Four sets of 25 seconds per shoulder. One set of 20 seconds per shoulder.

Workout Six: Five sets of 25 seconds per shoulder.

Workout Seven: One set of 30 seconds per shoulder. Four sets of 25 seconds per shoulder.

And so on.

I recommend capping this at five sets of 40 seconds per shoulder maximum, otherwise the volume becomes too much, and the effort level becomes too high.

Try to stay in the 20–40 second range if possible. This doesn't need to be exact, use the space and equipment you have available, but 20–40 seconds is a good place to be.

Exercise three is the sandbag box squat done for one all-out set.

End the day with direct work for the posterior chain and abs.

Monday: Sandbag Workout A

1. **Sandbag One-Motion Lift From The Ground To The Chest**
   - 5 single reps with 60–90 seconds rest between reps
2. **Sandbag Row**
   - 5–10 sets with 60–90 seconds rest between sets
3. **Sandbag Box Squat**

- 1 set
4. **Posterior Chain**
   - 100 reps
5. **Abs**
   - 100 reps
6. **Obliques**
   - 50 reps per side

Tuesday: Calisthenics Workout A

1. **Calisthenics Circuit:**
   - Neutral Pull-ups, Diamond Push-ups, Ab Wheel Rollouts (or hanging leg raises), Pike Push-ups
   - Rep Scheme: 6-5-4 done for rounds (20–25 minute range)
2. **Neck:**
   - Neck Curls + Neck Extensions
   - 4 sets of 25 reps each
3. **Forearms:**
   - Flexion Movement
   - Extension Movement
   - Supination Movement
   - Pronation Movement
   - Radial Deviation Movement
   - Ulnar Deviation Movement
   - 1 set to failure each in the 10–30 rep range
4. **Arms/Shoulders**
   - Bicep Curl + Tricep Extension + Shoulder Exercise
   - 2 sets to failure each in the 10–30 rep range
5. **Tricep Pushdowns**
   - 1 set of 100 reps

Wednesday: Off

Thursday: Sandbag Workout B

1. **Sandbag One-Motion Lift From The Ground To The Chest**
    - 5 single reps with 60–90 seconds rest between reps
2. **Sandbag Bear Hug Carry**
    - 5–10 sets with 60–90 seconds rest between sets
3. **Sandbag Box Squat**
    - 1 set
4. **Posterior Chain**
    - 100 reps
5. **Abs**
    - 100 reps
6. **Obliques**
    - 50 reps per side

Friday: Calisthenics Workout B

1. **Calisthenics Circuit:**
    - Pull-ups, Dips, Hanging Leg Raises, Decline Pike Push-ups
    - Rep Scheme: 5-3-2 done for rounds (20–25 minute range)
2. **Neck:**
    - Neck Curls + Neck Extensions
    - 4 sets of 25 reps each

3. **Forearms:**
   - Flexion Movement
   - Extension Movement
   - Supination Movement
   - Pronation Movement
   - Radial Deviation Movement
   - Ulnar Deviation Movement
   - 1 set to failure each in the 10–30 rep range
4. **Arms/Shoulders**
   - Bicep Curl + Tricep Extension + Shoulder Exercise
   - 2 sets to failure each in the 10–30 rep range
5. **Tricep Pushdowns**
   - 1 set of 100 reps

Saturday: Off

Sunday: Sandbag Workout C

1. **Sandbag One-Motion Lift From The Ground To The Chest**
   - 5 single reps with 60–90 seconds rest between reps
2. **Sandbag Shoulder Carry**
   - 5 sets per shoulder with 60–90 seconds rest between sets
3. **Sandbag Box Squat**
   - 1 set
4. **Posterior Chain**
   - 100 reps

5. **Abs**
    - 100 reps
6. **Obliques**
    - 50 reps per side

Monday: Calisthenics Workout A

Tuesday: Off

Wednesday: Sandbag Workout A

Thursday: Calisthenics Workout B

And so on.

If you need to train on the same days every week, use the following setup:

Week One:

- Monday: Sandbag Workout A
- Tuesday: Calisthenics Workout A
- Wednesday: Off
- Thursday: Sandbag Workout B
- Friday: Calisthenics Workout B
- Saturday: Off
- Sunday: Off

Week Two:

- Monday: Sandbag Workout C
- Tuesday: Calisthenics Workout A
- Wednesday: Off
- Thursday: Sandbag Workout A
- Friday: Calisthenics Workout B
- Saturday: Off
- Sunday: Off

Week Three:

- Monday: Sandbag Workout B
- Tuesday: Calisthenics Workout A
- Wednesday: Off
- Thursday: Sandbag Workout C
- Friday: Calisthenics Workout B
- Saturday: Off
- Sunday: Off

Repeat.

I Can Only Train Three Days Per Week

For this variation of the program, increase the length of each calisthenics circuit to 30–40 minutes.

Week One:
Monday: Sandbag Workout A

1. **Sandbag One-Motion Lift From The Ground To The Chest**
   - 5 single reps with 60–90 seconds rest between reps
2. **Sandbag Row**
   - 5–10 sets with 60–90 seconds rest between sets
3. **Sandbag Box Squat**
   - 1 set
4. **Posterior Chain**
   - 100 reps
5. **Abs**
   - 100 reps
6. **Obliques**
   - 50 reps per side

Tuesday: Off

Wednesday: Calisthenics Workout A

1. **Calisthenics Circuit:**
   - Neutral Pull-ups, Diamond Push-ups, Ab Wheel Rollouts (or hanging leg raises), Pike Push-ups
   - Rep Scheme: 6-5-4 done for rounds (30–40 minute range)
2. **Neck:**
   - Neck Curls + Neck Extensions
   - 4 sets of 25 reps each
3. **Forearms:**
   - Flexion Movement
   - Extension Movement

- Supination Movement
- Pronation Movement
- Radial Deviation Movement
- Ulnar Deviation Movement
- 1 set to failure each in the 10–30 rep range
4. **Arms/Shoulders**
    - Bicep Curl + Tricep Extension + Shoulder Exercise
    - 2 sets to failure each in the 10–30 rep range
5. **Tricep Pushdowns**
    - 1 set of 100 reps

Thursday: Off

Friday: Sandbag Workout B

1. **Sandbag One-Motion Lift From The Ground To The Chest**
    - 5 single reps with 60–90 seconds rest between reps
2. **Sandbag Bear Hug Carry**
    - 5–10 sets with 60–90 seconds rest between sets
3. **Sandbag Box Squat**
    - 1 set
4. **Posterior Chain**
    - 100 reps
5. **Abs**
    - 100 reps
6. **Obliques**
    - 50 reps per side

Saturday: Off

Sunday: Off

Week Two:
Monday: Sandbag Workout A

1. **Sandbag One-Motion Lift From The Ground To The Chest**
    - 5 single reps with 60–90 seconds rest between reps
2. **Sandbag Row**
    - 5–10 sets with 60–90 seconds rest between sets
3. **Sandbag Box Squat**
    - 1 set
4. **Posterior Chain**
    - 100 reps
5. **Abs**
    - 100 reps
6. **Obliques**
    - 50 reps per side

Tuesday: Off

Wednesday: Calisthenics Workout B

1. **Calisthenics Circuit:**
   - Pull-ups, Dips, Hanging Leg Raises, Decline Pike Push-ups
   - Rep Scheme: 5-3-2 done for rounds (30–40 minute range)
2. **Neck:**
   - Neck Curls + Neck Extensions
   - 4 sets of 25 reps each
3. **Forearms:**
   - Flexion Movement
   - Extension Movement
   - Supination Movement
   - Pronation Movement
   - Radial Deviation Movement
   - Ulnar Deviation Movement
   - 1 set to failure each in the 10–30 rep range
4. **Arms/Shoulders**
   - Bicep Curl + Tricep Extension + Shoulder Exercise
   - 2 sets to failure each in the 10–30 rep range
5. **Tricep Pushdowns**
   - 1 set of 100 reps

Thursday: Off

Friday: Sandbag Workout B

1. **Sandbag One-Motion Lift From The Ground To The Chest**
   - 5 single reps with 60–90 seconds rest between reps
2. **Sandbag Bear Hug Carry**
   - 5–10 sets with 60–90 seconds rest between sets
3. **Sandbag Box Squat**
   - 1 set
4. **Posterior Chain**
   - 100 reps
5. **Abs**
   - 100 reps
6. **Obliques**
   - 50 reps per side

Saturday: Off

Sunday: Off

Repeat.

I Want To Train Every Day

The program is easily adapted to a 'train every day' setup. The main change you'll want to make here is with the calisthenics circuits. Rather than 20–25 minutes, each circuit should last only 10–15 minutes. You'll also need more variety. It can be difficult to continue making progress long term with a circuit in the 10–15 minute range. For this reason, the program will rotate through four different circuits each week rather than two. You'll also need to pay very close attention to your records. If you fail to beat your previous record with a given circuit three attempts in a row, it's probably time to move on. Replace the circuit with a new one, and continue working with it for as long as you can until progress stops again.

Monday: Sandbag Workout A

1. **Sandbag One-Motion Lift From The Ground To The Chest**
    - 5 single reps with 60–90 seconds rest between reps
2. **Sandbag Row**
    - 5–10 sets with 60–90 seconds rest between sets
3. **Sandbag Box Squat**
    - 1 set
4. **Posterior Chain**
    - 100 reps
5. **Abs**
    - 100 reps
6. **Obliques**
    - 50 reps per side

Tuesday: Calisthenics Workout A

1. **Calisthenics Circuit:**
   - Neutral pull-ups, Diamond Push-ups, Ab Wheel Rollouts (or hanging leg raises), Pike Push-ups
   - Rep Scheme: 6-5-4 done for rounds (10–15 minute range)
2. **Neck:**
   - Neck Curls + Neck Extensions
   - 4 sets of 25 reps each
3. **Forearms:**
   - Flexion Movement
   - Extension Movement
   - Supination Movement
   - Pronation Movement
   - Radial Deviation Movement
   - Ulnar Deviation Movement
   - 1 set to failure each in the 10–30 rep range
4. **Arms/Shoulders**
   - Bicep Curl + Tricep Extension + Shoulder Exercise
   - 2 sets to failure each in the 10–30 rep range
5. **Tricep Pushdowns**
   - 1 set of 100 reps

Wednesday: Calisthenics Workout B

1. **Calisthenics Circuit:**
   - Pull-ups, Dips, Hanging Leg Raises, Decline Pike Push-ups
   - Rep Scheme: 5-3-2 done for rounds (10–15 minute range)

Thursday: Sandbag Workout B

1. **Sandbag One-Motion Lift From The Ground To The Chest**
   - 5 single reps with 60–90 seconds rest between reps
2. **Sandbag Bear Hug Carry**
   - 5–10 sets with 60–90 seconds rest between sets
3. **Sandbag Box Squat**
   - 1 set
4. **Posterior Chain**
   - 100 reps
5. **Abs**
   - 100 reps
6. **Obliques**
   - 50 reps per side

Friday: Calisthenics Workout C

1. **Calisthenics Circuit:**
   - Chin-ups, Decline Pike Push-ups, Ab Wheel Rollouts (or hanging leg raises), Decline Diamond Push-ups
   - Rep Scheme: 6-4-2 done for rounds (10–15 minute range)
2. **Neck:**
   - Neck Curls + Neck Extensions
   - 4 sets of 25 reps each
3. **Forearms:**
   - Flexion Movement
   - Extension Movement

- Supination Movement
- Pronation Movement
- Radial Deviation Movement
- Ulnar Deviation Movement
- 1 set to failure each in the 10–30 rep range
4. **Arms/Shoulders**
    - Bicep Curl + Tricep Extension + Shoulder Exercise
    - 2 sets to failure each in the 10–30 rep range
5. **Tricep Pushdowns**
    - 1 set of 100 reps

Saturday: Calisthenics Workout D

1. **Calisthenics Circuit:**
    - Inverted Rows, Dips, Hanging Leg Raises, Pike Push-ups
    - Rep Scheme: 8-6-4 done for rounds (10–15 minute range)

Sunday: Active Recovery

Nothing overly taxing.
Use Sunday to prepare yourself for the week ahead.
Here are a few ideas for the day:
Rebounding
Jump rope
Animal movement
Light band work
Rucking

Yoga
Hiking

Repeat.

All-Out Sets Twice Every Week Are You Crazy?

It's been my experience that a higher frequency actually makes each individual set of box squats seem like less of a big deal. The mind will condition itself to the work when given the opportunity. That said, twice a week might be too much for some. That's okay, there's an easy workaround.

For this variation of the program, replace box squats in "Sandbag Workout B" with the basic lift from the lap to the chest.

For this exercise we'll use short rest times and focus on training density. This setup feels very similar to a set of high-rep box squats, but isn't quite as mentally taxing.

How To: To perform the exercise, bring a sandbag to your lap, hold onto it with a bear hug grip, stand up, drop back down, and repeat.

Weight: Choose a weight that would challenge you for an all-out set in the 6–10 rep range.

Reps: Start with 3 reps per set.

Sets: Complete ten sets with 45 seconds rest between sets.

Progression: The total number of sets will not change over time. Every workout, add an additional rep to one of the sets.

Example:
(Chosen sandbag weight would challenge you for an all-out set in the 6–10 rep range)

Workout One: 10 sets
(Reps)
3, 3, 3, 3, 3, 3, 3, 3, 3, 3

Workout Two: 10 sets
(Reps)
4, 3, 3, 3, 3, 3, 3, 3, 3, 3

Workout Three: 10 sets
(Reps)
4, 4, 3, 3, 3, 3, 3, 3, 3, 3

Workout Four: 10 sets
(Reps)
4, 4, 4, 3, 3, 3, 3, 3, 3, 3

Workout Five: 10 sets
(Reps)
4, 4, 4, 4, 3, 3, 3, 3, 3, 3

And so on.

Continue in this way until you reach ten sets of 5 reps. Once you reach that point, add weight and start over at ten sets of 3 reps.

Note: Place your sandbag on a platform between sets.

Monday: Sandbag Workout A

1. **Sandbag One-Motion Lift From The Ground To The Chest**
    - 5 single reps with 60–90 seconds rest between reps
2. **Sandbag Row**
    - 5–10 sets with 60–90 seconds rest between sets
3. **Sandbag Box Squat**
    - 1 set
4. **Posterior Chain**
    - 100 reps
5. **Abs**
    - 100 reps

6. **Obliques**
    - 50 reps per side

Tuesday: Calisthenics Workout A

1. **Calisthenics Circuit:**
    - Neutral Pull-ups, Diamond Push-ups, Ab Wheel Rollouts (or hanging leg raises), Pike Push-ups
    - Rep Scheme: 6-5-4 done for rounds (20–25 minute range)
2. **Neck:**
    - Neck Curls + Neck Extensions
    - 4 sets of 25 reps each
3. **Forearms:**
    - Flexion Movement
    - Extension Movement
    - Supination Movement
    - Pronation Movement
    - Radial Deviation Movement
    - Ulnar Deviation Movement
    - 1 set to failure each in the 10–30 rep range
4. **Arms/Shoulders**
    - Bicep Curl + Tricep Extension + Shoulder Exercise
    - 2 sets to failure each in the 10–30 rep range
5. **Tricep Pushdowns**
    - 1 set of 100 reps

Wednesday: Off

Thursday: Sandbag Workout B

1. **Sandbag One-Motion Lift From The Ground To The Chest**
   - 5 single reps with 60–90 seconds rest between reps
2. **Sandbag Bear Hug Carry**
   - 5–10 sets with 60–90 seconds rest between sets
3. **Sandbag Lift From The Lap To The Chest**
   - 10 sets with 45 seconds rest between sets
4. **Posterior Chain**
   - 100 reps
5. **Abs**
   - 100 reps
6. **Obliques**
   - 50 reps per side

Friday: Calisthenics Workout B

1. **Calisthenics Circuit:**
   - Pull-ups, Dips, Hanging Leg Raises, Decline Pike Push-ups
   - Rep Scheme: 5-3-2 done for rounds (20–25 minute range)
2. **Neck:**
   - Neck Curls + Neck Extensions
   - 4 sets of 25 reps each
3. **Forearms:**
   - Flexion Movement
   - Extension Movement
   - Supination Movement

- Pronation Movement
- Radial Deviation Movement
- Ulnar Deviation Movement
- 1 set to failure each in the 10–30 rep range
4. **Arms/Shoulders**
    - Bicep Curl + Tricep Extension + Shoulder Exercise
    - 2 sets to failure each in the 10–30 rep range
5. **Tricep Pushdowns**
    - 1 set of 100 reps

Saturday: Off

Sunday: Off

Repeat.

ABOUT THE AUTHOR

Cody Janko is the Amazon best-selling author of *Sandbag Hypertrophy*. Also known as The Stone Circle on YouTube, he is an NCCA accredited Certified Personal Trainer with well over a decade of lifting experience.

When he's not busy at his day job working with rescue dogs, you're likely to find Cody somewhere along the forest path searching for a good stone to lift.

ENDNOTES

1 Strossen, Randall. *Super Squats: How to Gain 30 Pounds of Muscle in 6 Weeks.* IronMind Enterprises, 1989.

2 Staley, Charles. *Muscle Logic: Escalating Density Training.* Rodale Books, 2005.

3 Kubik, Brooks. *Dinosaur Training: Lost Secrets of Strength and Development.* Brooks D. Kubik, 1996.